PROFIT FIRST

FOR

TRADIES

TRANSFORM YOUR BUSINESS FROM A CASH EATING MONSTER TO A MONEY MAKING MACHINE

KATIE CRISMALE-MARSHALL

FOREWORD BY MIKE MICHALOWICZ

'Tradies are central to the Australian economy. Yet far too many are coming undone due to cash flow issues. But, as Katie captures so well, this doesn't have to be the case. All because one of the most important tools in their arsenal is, in fact, learning how to manage their finances.

'And from a client's perspective, when given the choice between paying on the spot thanks to clever tech or chasing up bills for months to come – there's no questioning what wins. All the more proof that it's not only time for tradies to put profit first, but to harness all of the technology at their disposal.'

Trent Innes – Managing Director, Xero Australia and Asia

'I think this book, *Profit First for Tradies*, is going to be an absolute life changer for a lot of tradies.'

Clinton Cowin – Managing Director TradiePad

'There is no doubt that being a tradie is tough. And that's what I love about everything that Katie Crismale-Marshall does. She gets the struggle, she provides smart strategies and practical advice designed to take the financial stress out of being a tradie, and she's not afraid to call it the way it is. This is a must read book for every tradie in the country.'

Andrew Griffiths – Australia's #1 Small Business Author, Global Speaker

'Being a business owner can be a struggle when you don't have the right tools. Even more so for our tradies who are exceptional crafts-people yet have rarely been shown how to run a profitable business. As a result, they have a constant battle with their cash flow, which is a battle they rarely win. In her book *Profit First for Tradies*, Katie has clearly identified the steps tradies need to take in order to turn their business around and run a profitable trades business.'

Daniel Priestley – Co-Founder of DENT, Author of Oversubscribed, 24 Assets, Entrepreneur Revolution *and* Key Person of Influence

'Most business owners work hard for everyone except themselves. In particular, tradies do a wonderful job supporting the community and yet are often working for less than minimum wage. This is a definitive book to show them a pathway for how they can not only serve their clients but look after their families for years to come.'

Dr David Dugan – Business Coach & Mentor

ACKNOWLEDGEMENTS

I believe business is a team sport, and without a great team around you business is hard, very hard. You must take one step at a time to keep moving forward.

You also need great examples of business owners who are doing things differently and having a positive impact on the business world and the world in general to show you opportunities you never realised were possible – like writing a book.

It all started about five years ago when my brother Jamie suggested I listen to Franziska and Christo's podcast. They are the amazing founders of Basic Bananas. The first podcast I listened to was an interview with Glen Carlson talking about his Key Person of Influence (KPI) program. Within minutes of listening to the interview I had Googled KPI and had registered for their one-day business event.

It was during this day that I first saw Andrew Griffiths speak on the stage along with a handful of other exceptional speakers. By the end of the day I had signed up for the KPI program – and had no idea at the time how much of an impact it would have on me as a businesswoman.

Fast forward a few years and an email to Andrew asking him for advice on how to write a book was the start of my writing. Thank you Andrew for being my brilliant writing coach who stepped me through the writing process to make what I thought would be a very trying process extremely enjoyable. Dare I say … it was fun.

Through the KPI program I began to look at business differently, and it was one of the mentors, Dr David Dugan, who first introduced me to Profit First. It was also through this program that I met Michael Hanrahan from Michael Hanrahan Publishing.

From my first phone call with Michael once I had decided to write this book, he and his team have been incredible to deal with. The entire publishing process was so simple. Michael and his team stepped me through every step, making sure I had a clear list of what I needed to do and by when. This certainly took away the stress of self-publishing.

In another chance encounter a few years ago I was fortunate to be introduced to Laura Elkaslassy, who at the time was a certified Profit First Professional. At that stage I was implementing Profit First in my own business, and had some questions which she very kindly answered for me.

I had decided to become certified in Profit First and started my training through homebase (Profit First head office US) when Laura and my paths crossed again. Laura had now taken on the role as CEO of Profit First Australia, and was to become my mentor through my certification process. Thank you Laura for your support, encouragement and most importantly every time you have challenged me on an idea. It has certainly helped push me outside my comfort zone and helped me grow to be a better businesswoman. Without your confidence in me to write this book I am not sure I would have taken on this challenge.

And finally, thank you to Mike Michalowicz for not only bringing your Profit First system to life through your *Profit First* book but most importantly for your casual comment over lunch during our mastermind day suggesting that I could write the tradies version of *Profit First*. As soon as you mentioned writing the book, I knew in my gut that I had to do it. I knew our Aussie tradies needed this book now more than ever.

Disclaimer
The material in this publication is of the nature of general comment only, and does
not represent professional advice. It is not intended to provide specific guidance for
particular circumstances and it should not be relied on as the basis for any decision
to take action or not take action on any matter which it covers. Readers should
obtain professional advice where appropriate, before making any such decision.
To the maximum extent permitted by law, the author and publisher disclaim all
responsibility and liability to any person, arising directly or indirectly from any
person taking or not taking action based on the information in this publication.

CONTENTS

CONTENTS

FOREWORD

By Mike Michalowicz

I was at an energy rich, get stuff done meetup with Profit First Professionals (PFPs) in Melbourne. This is a collection of the leading Australian experts in the Profit First method. The CEO of Profit First Professionals is Laura Elkaslassy, and she had coordinated a day of learning and sharing best practices across industries. For example, what expertise could PFPs serving the retail store industry share to help PFPs serving online ecommerce markets? She smartly directed us to mix up during our lunch session. She wanted people who hadn't had the opportunity to connect yet to spend time sharing their own unique expertise. My seatmate? Katie Crismale-Marshall.

The standard 'get to know each other better' question is, 'What do you do?' But since I already knew that, I went with the advanced version of that question: 'What is something that you know inside and out that would surprise other people?' The response: 'Engine repair.'

Katie went on to explain her experience in working with cars, boats and motorcycles. She knew the mechanics. She had a passion

1

for it. She even had her own paddock basher (which, being an American, I hadn't a clue what she was talking about – we call those things 'beaters' or 'hunk-o-junks') that she would race around in and repair when it wasn't working. Her father was a motor mechanic by trade and sparked Katie's passion. But it was more than just her dad, it was her whole family who were in the trades. She grew up on this stuff, and married into it too (her husband is in the trades too).

The trades are what Katie knows. She knows the importance of the work. And she is passionate about the tradie community.

'There is an art to mechanics. Just as there is an art to all of the trades,' she explained. 'The people in the trades space spend years, if not decades, mastering their craft.'

She continued, 'And they are never done. They are constantly learning how to work with the newest electrical systems, or the newest heating and cooling machinery, or the newly designed engines. The trades are made of people who are constantly learning and innovating to make our world a more efficient and better place.'

If you paint walls or build the walls. If you install electric systems or plumbing systems. If you repair cars or build them. No matter what trade you are in, the world depends on you. You are the foundation to human comfort and convenience. We need you, badly.

But the only way for us to experience the services you deliver is for you to be profitable.

Sadly, the majority of tradies struggle with profit. Their businesses are limping along. And, as you will see in Katie's introduction, people in the trades are questioning if they will even make it.

Even make it? Even make it? Are you kidding me? The businesses humanity depends on are on the verge of going under. Something is seriously wrong here. But there is good news. In this book you will find the solution to your financial challenges. You are going to discover the way to become permanently profitable.

The irony is your clients want you to be profitable. They want you to be wildly profitable. They will never say to you 'please charge me more' or 'please bump up your prices on me'. But they will say they want the best of you. They want your focus. They want you to deliver all you can for them.

They want to know that you are not distracted. They want to know you are not worrying about how you are going to get that next client in the door and the next dollar in your pocket. And the only way to serve your clients the way they want to be served is to ensure you are not worrying about money. In other words, you must be profitable.

This book is your guide to achieving just that.

I am honoured to introduce you to Katie Crismale-Marshall, my friend and the leading expert in profitability for tradies. The small investment of time that it takes for you to read the book and implement what Katie teaches will return to you with a permanent profit stream. To say this book is life changing is an understatement. It is life saving.

I wish you a wonderful journey as you grow the profits in your business. I typically would say here that I also wish you luck in the journey, but there is no need for that. You don't need luck, you have the entire system in your hands as we speak. Just do it. Just do Profit First.... tradie style!

INTRODUCTION

'I'M NOT SURE MY BUSINESS WILL MAKE IT'

It was an email from a new bookkeeping tradie client, Jack, who is a builder, that read:

> I'm sorry to bother you. I'm not sure my
> business will make it. I'm not sure if you can
> help but I don't know what to do now.

The email had been sent at 4:08 am that morning, and I recognised the desperation. It was not the first message I'd received like this, but this one really had an impact on me. It made me wonder how many other tradies were being kept awake by the same thoughts? How many tradies don't know who to turn to for help? How many families are suffering because their tradie is so stressed they can barely function?

And what about my tradie relatives and friends: were they too at this stage?

I organised a chat with Jack that same morning. From the outside he looked like he had everything sorted: he had plenty of jobs on the go, he had great turnover, a staff of five, and some specialist subbies on the various jobs – yet at the end of each and every week Jack still had the same question: how am I going to pay all the bills, because I don't have enough cash in the bank?

Like many tradies, his business looked great from the outside, yet the majority of them struggle with cash flow.

Why is that?

Over the years, what I have realised is that when it comes to paying the bills, tradies like Jack struggle week in and week out and it is slowly and silently suffocating them. Week in and week out their mind races while they try to guess who will pay their invoice on time for them to have money to pay their staff, their subbies and their bills, and maybe – just maybe – there will be some left over for them to take as well.

Cash flow, or lack thereof, is slowly destroying their business – and them.

This conversation with Jack flicked a switch for me. I realised my bookkeeping business, Efficient Tradie, wasn't having the impact I thought and hoped it was. I had to do something else, something *more*.

SHOCKED BUT NOT SURPRISED

At this stage of business I had various clients across various industries, and it was this email from Jack that made me really consider the impact that lack of cash flow was having on my other tradie clients.

I created a survey with one simple question:

Are you kept up at night worrying about your cash flow?

The survey could be completed anonymously, and I sent it out to all my tradie clients that day.

Every single response came back yes.

I was shocked, but not surprised.

I have been surrounded by tradies my entire life, with some of my earliest memories being playing in the sand at my grandparents' concrete factory and playing in the shed with my dad while he rebuilt motors for the car or boat. My uncles and brother are tradies, my husband has two trades, and my father in law and brother in laws are also tradies.

Some of my fondest memories are of sitting in the shed at Dargle while my dad and his mates worked to all hours of the morning to get a motor together so they could race in the Bridge to Bridge or the circuit races held on the Hawkesbury River. If I wasn't sitting in the shed watching motors being built, I was wandering around the shed at Child Play Marine watching Rob and Gary Newall with dad lending a hand to build ski boats and some of the fastest circuit boats in Australia.

Being fortunate to grow up on acres on the banks of the Hawkesbury River at Lower Portland also meant I had to be resourceful if my motorbike stopped working or my paddock basher decided it didn't want to go any further. I often had to figure out myself what could possibly be wrong before I could go to dad with my list of potential problems for help, at which point he would teach me how to fix it. I've always loved pulling things apart and putting them back together again, although my parents were not pleased to find me in the shed one day where I had stripped my new BMX down to the frame. I had put thought into it first though, and I had pulled open a cardboard box and traced around each part as I took it off the bike to ensure I had a plan to put it back together again. I've always been a planner, so it seems.

Yet as I think back on the conversations I overheard while I was growing up, and have continued to have as an adult with my tradie friends and family about their businesses, I realised many of them could have sent me this same email.

This had been going on for years and years for our tradies, and it had become the norm to have cash flow issues. There had to be a solution, and I had to find it.

I had been introduced to the book *Profit First* by Mike Michalowicz in 2015, the year after Mike wrote it, and I ordered myself a copy. When it arrived I promptly read it from cover to cover, and then put it on my bookcase with my collection of various well-read business books. I didn't take any action at this stage as I had been in business for a little over three years and was still focused on building my cloud bookkeeping business, Efficient Tradie. I thought my strength and how I could make the biggest difference was helping tradies set up efficient bookkeeping system using Xero and HubDoc.

While I was successful at doing this with my clients, and for the first time my clients actually had access to up-to-date data about their business and they knew exactly what their business was and wasn't making, I soon realised efficient bookkeeping wasn't the answer – it was only part of the puzzle. I thought if I helped tradies organise their numbers into a nice efficient system like Xero, it would be easy for them to know and understand their numbers and make better decisions with their money, which would lead to them solving their cash flow issues.

I was wrong, and this email from Jack proved that to me.

SHE'LL BE RIGHT

Being surrounded by tradies has meant I was often able to watch and learn from what they were doing. As I grew older and our family friends and then my own tradie friends moved into having their own businesses, I also saw firsthand just how hard it was for them to have successful businesses. Working 60-plus hours per week and still struggling with cash flow was tough to watch; still, when I offered to help they maintained it would be okay eventually. I was often met with comments such as, 'Nah, it's okay – I was talking to James and he is going through the same thing. It'll work itself out.'

The 'she'll be right' attitude is especially strong in our tradies, even when they are struggling. I was astounded that even though I had been around tradies my entire life, I'd missed the biggest issue they were all having until now. The recognition of the 'she'll be right attitude' and the 'I can fix it myself' attitude I had seen all my life made me realise that it was very difficult for our tradies to reach out and ask for help, even when they were struggling as much as they were.

Prior to having my children, I was a financial planner who worked with mostly small business owners, and unfortunately I saw many business owners who were ten or so years out from retirement and had very little to show for it. Even though their business had provided them with a job and income for all those years, it never provided them with profit. I had this grand dream that I would help my clients with their bookkeeping and miraculously they would have spare money and would be able to plan to invest some money and plan for their retirement.

My dream of helping tradies have a better life in retirement all because I helped them sort out their bookkeeping was, on reflection, ridiculous.

If only it was that simple.

THE MISSING PIECE

I soon realised I had fallen into the same trap as my tradies, and we were all headed down the same road my self-employed financial planning clients had been on.

As I looked for a solution for my tradies, I reviewed my own business too. My business had always been able to provide me with what I needed from it – at this stage all I wanted was a wage to help contribute to our household expenses. I diligently kept my bookkeeping up to date with Xero, making it easy, yet come the end of the year when my tax was done my profit and loss showed the elusive profit yet my bank account was not looking as healthy as my profit and loss led me to believe. I was left wondering where I had gone wrong; my bookkeeping was impeccable and up to date, yet I didn't have much to show for my work.

I had heard this story time and time again from my new tradie clients. They spoke openly of the dreaded meeting with the accountant to do their end-of-year tax, only to have the profit and loss and balance sheet slide across the desk at them. As they flick through the reports, the echo of the accountant's words rings through their head: 'Congratulations, you have made a profit'. And each and every one of them had told me their first thoughts were always a variation of: 'How is that possible? I don't have that amount of money in the bank and I have a stack of bills still to be paid.' As they sit silently in the accountant's office and finally catch their thoughts, they for another year thank the accountant, pay their bill, and walk out the door having no idea what happened to that profit the accountant is talking about.

I have had that same experience. I realised I may be self-employed, but what I had was a job with the added stress of being a business owner, and worse still I was not getting rewarded at all for taking the risk of being in business.

There was no profit in my business.

I realised there was a missing piece to my financial puzzle, just like there was for Jack who sent me that early morning email.

Neither of us had a cash management system.

I needed something simple to follow for my tradies to even consider it. While cash flow issues are the number one cause of stress for most businesses, it is especially common for tradies. They are busy getting the work and getting the jobs done. They would need something that makes sense to them and that we could implement without too many complicated spreadsheets or boring graphs.

As I sat at my desk staring past my computer screen, attempting to find a solution, I spotted *Profit First* on my bookcase staring back at me.

I kicked myself for not thinking of it sooner.

I took the time over that weekend to reread *Profit First*, but this time I took notes and more notes and more notes, so I could implement Profit First in my business, first to make sure it worked, and secondly so I could see if it would work with my tradies. As I worked through the book taking my notes, I realised there would need to be some adjustments made to suit businesses here in Australia. I reached out to Laura Elkaslassy, who was a certified Profit First Professional in Australia and is now the CEO of Profit First Australia, to 'run a few things by her'. Laura was instrumental in giving me the push I needed to finally implement Profit First in my own business. Little did I know where this push would take me, and how my Profit First journey would help me help so many tradies and their families.

I had realised I was on the path my self-employed financial planning clients had travelled, and I had the experience to know where it led: to struggling in retirement. I could no longer stand by and watch my family, friends and clients struggle with cash flow. Profit First could be the answer to so many sleepless nights that everyone was suffering, mostly in silence.

First thing Monday morning I Googled 'fee-free business banking', and opened up my bank accounts with BankWest, the only bank at the time that wasn't charging monthly account-keeping fees. I opened the five foundational Profit First bank accounts: Income, Profit, Owner's Compensation (Owner's Comp), Tax and Operating Expenses (Opex) accounts. I also opened up another bank account for GST. I changed my invoices to be paid into the income account, and set my day each week when I would do my allocations.

My Profit First journey had begun, and what a journey it continues to be.

HOW DO YOU GET THE MOST OUT OF THIS BOOK?

I have broken this book into four parts: Profit, Plan, Prepare and Prosper. These are the four sections you will need to work on to get your business on track to becoming profitable and the business you have dreamed of having. Each part has a different focus, and should be thought of like the foundation of your business. If you don't put all the piers in as per the plans, the house won't last.

My biggest tip for this book is to not get overwhelmed if you feel like you are trying to do too many things at once. You can't fix everything all at once, and this is a marathon not a sprint. This book is the best coach you can have. Throughout the book I have stepped you through each stage in the order I have for a reason. Please don't skip reading any sections, otherwise you may find yourself a little lost. Think of this book as your map, and the easiest way to the treasure – in this case, profit – is to just follow this map.

You may move through some sections more quickly than others depending on where your business is now and where you want to be, and you may have to come back to redo sections again (or maybe even more than once), and that is okay. This book is also written for whichever stage you are at in your business, and the beauty of it is that as your business changes you can always come back to this book and review your situation again against this map.

So, let's get into it …

Part I

PROFIT

Chapter 1

THE CORE PRINCIPLES OF PROFIT FIRST

As a tradie, have you ever experienced:

- ☐ working excessive hours
- ☐ working weekends
- ☐ missing out on family events
- ☐ never or rarely going on holidays
- ☐ if you do go on holidays, you can't switch off because your business still needs you
- ☐ working for clients that you don't want to work for but you 'need the money'
- ☐ regretting taking on that job for that client
- ☐ losing money on jobs because the client is being difficult

- ☐ having clients who are late payers

- ☐ having clients who are *really* late payers

- ☐ having clients who just don't pay you at all

- ☐ wasting time following up the abovementioned slow/late/not paying clients

- ☐ feeling like you just can't get ahead

- ☐ owing money to the Australian Taxation Office (ATO)

- ☐ owing money for superannuation

- ☐ feeling like you would earn more money if you 'just got a job'

- ☐ having your employed friends thinking that because you are self-employed you are 'rolling in it'

- ☐ not knowing why it is so hard

- ☐ thinking you should have been able to turn your business around by now

- ☐ not knowing how you got to this point?

These issues are extremely common among the tradies I work with. Most of them are dedicated and hardworking, yet they still can't seem to get ahead because they don't know how to properly address these issues. Often they think the answer is simply to work harder, but if the structure of your business is fundamentally flawed then working harder is not going to help.

Because you're reading this book I'm going to assume that you are experiencing some or many of these – or even *all* of them. In this and subsequent chapters I'm going to show you the issues you need to address in your business to solve these common problems once and for all, and give you a system to ensure sustainable success in your business.

UNDERSTANDING CASH FLOW

Let's start by looking at cash flow. 'Cash is king' is a common phrase in the business world; without cash in the bank it becomes impossible to pay your bills and keep your business alive. Without enough cash in the bank, tradies often turn to credit to get them through, or they use money that has been collected for GST and is owed the ATO to help them get out of a cash flow bind, thinking they can 'sort it out later'. Most businesses that go out of business do so because they have used up all their cash, they have poor cash flow, and they are maxed out all the credit they have been able to get.

Unfortunately, in Australia it has been fairly easy for tradies to get leases, loans, overdrafts and credit cards in recent years, and although the rules around lending have tightened up lately there are still more tradies than I would like to imagine who have excessive revolving credit at their disposal. The problem with using credit to 'get them through' is that they never get off the credit treadmill.

As a result, I see too many tradies who continue to put their head in the sand and ignore the very real cash flow crisis they are facing, which is putting their business at great risk. What I have found is they often do this because they don't know where to turn for a solution. It seems like everyone around them is doing well and they are the only ones who are failing (as they see it). This plays havoc with their self-esteem and only makes the problem worse.

One of the keys to successfully managing your cash flow is creating and sticking to a rhythm. We will hear more from Mike about enforcing a rhythm on page 24. (Throughout the book sections from Mike's book will be shaded as follows. They are, of course, used with Mike's permission.)

SO HOW DO WE ENFORCE A RHYTHM?

Just as it keeps us from starving and bingeing on food, enforcing a rhythm works with money, too. When we get into a rhythm we don't get into the reactive mode of crazy spending when we get big deposits and panicking in the face of big cash dips. I am not saying the money will automatically appear and you'll always have cash at your disposal, but establishing a rhythm will get you out of the daily panic. In fact, establishing a rhythm will also be a great indicator of overall cash flow. This system is the easiest way to measure cash flow. Instead of reading the cash flow statement (which, honestly, when was the last time you did that?), you can measure your cash flow by just checking your bank accounts, which you do anyway.

When you get into a rhythm with your cash management you'll have your finger on the pulse of your business. You will monitor your cash position every day by just looking at your bank account. Log in. Spend two seconds looking at your balances. Log out. You will know where you stand that quickly. Think of your cash flow as waves rolling onto the beach. If the cash wave is big, you will notice and take action (this is when looking at the reports with the guidance of a pro is helpful). When the waves are small, you will surely notice that, too. Most of the time, I expect the cash waves will be normal, and no action will be required. But no matter what, you will always know. Because you will continue to do what you normally do: log into your bank account.

One of the many advantages of Profit First is it's a framework that can be used as is for many different business types. It can also be tailored for a specific industry such as tradies, so that it can be even more beneficial for them and their specific industry needs.

The four core principles as described in *Profit First* remain the same; they are the foundation on which *Profit First for Tradies* is built. For those who haven't read *Profit First* or who need a refresher, here are those core principles as they are in Profit First.

THE FOUR CORE PRINCIPLES OF PROFIT FIRST

Let's take a moment to talk dietary science. No groans, please. This stuff is fascinating.

In 2012, a report by Koert Van Ittersum and Brian Wansink in the *Journal of Consumer Research* concluded that the average plate size in America had grown 23% between the years 1900 and 2012, from 9.6 inches to 11.8 inches. Running the math, the article explains that should this increase in plate size encourage an individual to consume just fifty more calories per day, that person would put on an extra five pounds of weight each year. Year after year, that adds up to a very chunky monkey.

But using smaller plates is just one factor. A Twinkie on a small plate is still a Twinkie. There is more to a healthy diet, and it is based on four core principles of weight loss and nutrition.

1. **Use small plates:** Using smaller plates starts a chain reaction. When you use a small plate, you get smaller portions, which means you take in fewer calories. When you take in fewer calories than you normally would, you start to lose weight.

2. **Serve sequentially:** If you eat the vegetables, rich in nutrients and vitamins, first, they will start satisfying your hunger. When you move on to the next course – your mac and cheese or mashed potatoes (they don't count as veggies!) – you will automatically eat less. By changing the sequence of your meals by eating your vegetables first, you automatically bring a nutritional balance to your diet.

3. **Remove temptation:** Remove any temptation from where you eat. People are driven by convenience. If you're anything like me, when there's a bag of Doritos sitting in the kitchen, it calls out to you constantly – even when you aren't hungry. If you don't have any junk food in the house, you're probably not going to run out to the store to get it. (That would mean

putting on pants.) You're going to eat the healthy food you stocked instead.

4. **Enforce a rhythm:** If you wait until you are hungry to eat, it is already too late and you will binge. Then you are likely to eat too much and stuff yourself. You go from starving to stuffed, and back to starving again. These peaks and valleys in your hunger result in way too much calorie consumption. Instead, eat regularly (many researchers suggest five small meals a day) so that you never get hungry. Without the peaks and valleys, you will actually eat fewer calories.

Though they don't realise it, the folks in the diet industry know quite a lot about growing a healthy business.

Let's examine these principles one by one:

1. Parkinson's Law: why your business is like a tube of toothpaste

In the years since I discovered these four physical health principles, I dug further and further into why they matter. The four principles that PBS fitness expert shared are all rooted in behavioural science. When you know what makes you tick, it gives you a massive advantage over yourself. Behavioral science gives you the advantage to subdue your biggest competitor, namely you.

Let's start with small plates. In 1955, a modern philosopher named C. Northcote Parkinson came up with the counterintuitive Parkinson's Law: that the demand for something expands to match its supply. In economics, this is called induced demand – it's why expanding roads to reduce traffic congestion never works in the long term because more drivers always show up in their cars to fill those extra lanes. In other words, if you went to a Spanish tapas bar that served those tiny plates, you would eat less. But if you went to a Ponderosa all-you-can eat buffet, where they have plates the size of manhole covers, you would eat until the food was coming out your ears. (It's an all-you-CAN-eat buffet. . . . Challenge accepted!)

Similarly, if your client gives you a week to turn around a project, you'd likely take the whole week – but if she gives you just a day, you'll make it happen in a day. You see, the more we have of something, the more of it we consume. This is true for anything: food, time, even toothpaste.

How much toothpaste do you use when you have a brand-new tube of toothpaste? A big ol' glop of it, right? I mean, why not? After all, you have a full tube of toothpaste. So you put a nice long bead on that brush of yours. Then before you start brushing, you turn on the faucet to moisten up the brush a little. Then it happens... damn it, the paste falls into the sink. But who cares, right? You just opened up that tube, for God's sake! You have tons of this stuff. So you put on another big ol' glop and brush away.

But when you open that cabinet drawer and find a nearly empty tube...my oh my, how the game changes. It starts off with an insane amount of squeezing, twisting, and turning. You reach for your toothbrush, momentarily releasing a little bit of your vice like grip on the tube, and with that, like a tortoise's head when a three-year-old comes at it with a stick, the paste shoots back into the tube. You could shout out some expletives at this point, but you can't because you are already onto stage 2 of toothpaste extraction: biting down hard on the tube. With a precarious balance of biting, one hand squeezing and tube twisting, while your other hand somehow tries to get the brush bristles to scoop out toothpaste, you have a victory. One droplet of toothpaste. Which is just enough for that fresh-mouth sensation.

Isn't it funny how much we change based upon what is available? Here is what's fascinating: Parkinson's Law triggers two behaviors when supply is scant. When you have less, you do two things. The first is obvious: you become frugal. When there is less toothpaste in the tube, you use less to brush your teeth. That is the obvious part. But something else, far more impactful happens: you become extremely innovative and find all sorts of ways to extract that last drop of toothpaste from the tube.

If there is one thing that will forever change your relationship with money, it is the understanding of Parkinson's Law. You need to intentionally make less toothpaste (money) available to brush your teeth (to operate your business). When there is less, you will automatically run your business more frugally (that's good) and you will run your business far more innovatively (that's great!).

If you first extract your profit and remove it from sight, you'll be left with a nearly empty toothpaste tube to run your business. When less money is available to run your business, you will find ways to get the same or better results with less. By taking your profit first, you will be forced to think smarter and innovate more.

2. The Primacy Effect: why the first part of profit first matters

The second behavioral principle you need to understand about yourself is called the Primacy Effect. The principle is this: we place additional significance on whatever we encounter first. Here's a little demonstration that may help you understand.

I am going to show you two sets of words. One set describes a sinner and another describes a saint. The goal is, as quickly as possible, to determine which one is which. Got it? Good. Now look at the two sets of words below and determine which one describes the sinner and which one the saint.

1. EVIL, HATE, ANGER, JOY, CARE, LOVE

2. LOVE, CARE, JOY, ANGER, HATE, EVIL

At first glance you likely identified the first set of words to be the sinner and the second set of words to be the saint. If you did, that is wonderful news, because it means you are a human being and are experiencing the Primacy Effect. In other words, you will thrive under Profit First. If you tried to figure out the catch as you were going through the exercise, that is awesome news, too; it means you are an entrepreneur and are more than willing to break old systems (like reading left to right only), which also means you will thrive under Profit First.

Now look at the set of words again. You will see that both sets of words are identical, just in the opposite sequence.

So when you see EVIL and HATE at the start of a set of words, your mind assigns greater weight to those words and less weight to the remaining words. When the set started with LOVE and CARE you put the weight there.

When we follow the conventional formula of Sales – Expenses = Profit, we are primed to focus on those first two words, Sales and Expenses, and treat Profit as an afterthought. We then behave accordingly. We sell as hard as we can, then use the money we collect to pay expenses. We stay stuck in the cycle of selling to pay bills, over and over again, wondering why we never see any profit. Who's the sinner now?

When profit comes first, it is the focus, and it is never forgotten.

3. Remove temptation: once you take your profit first, put it away

My greatest weakness is Chocodiles: Twinkies covered in dark chocolate, filled with cream, and wrapped in love. Fortunately, they stopped making them.[1] But if one sneaked into my house, even if it had expired in 1972, I would devour that delicious elixir of love and monounsaturated fats. Now I always make sure I have healthy options with me, and the junk is nowhere around.

Money works the same way. As you implement Profit First, you are going to use the powerful force of 'out of sight, out of mind.' As you generate a profit (which, remember, starts today), you are going to remove the money from your immediate access. You won't see it,

---

1   For my Chocodile loving comrades: supposedly Hostess has reintroduced the product, albeit slightly reformulated. Distribution is sparse, yet I have got my hands on a few. If these are the new formula, they taste like they have been on the shelf since 1972…and they are still delicious.

so you won't access it. And just like anything that you don't have a reasonable degree of access to, you will find a way to work with what you do have and not worry about what you don't. Then, when Mr. Buffett (ahem, your profit account) releases money to you, it will serve as a bonus.

4. Enforce a rhythm

Just as it keeps us from starving and bingeing on food, enforcing a rhythm works with money, too. When we get into a rhythm, we don't get into the reactive mode of crazy spending when we get big deposits and panicking in the face of big cash dips. I am not saying the money will automatically appear and you'll always have cash at your disposal, but establishing a rhythm will get you out of the daily panic.

In fact, establishing a rhythm will also be a great indicator of overall cash flow. This system is the easiest way to measure cash flow. Instead of reading the cash flow statement (which, honestly, when was the last time you did that?), you can measure your cash flow by just checking your bank accounts, which you do anyway.

When you get into a rhythm with your cash management you'll have your finger on the pulse of your business. You will monitor your cash position every day by just looking at your bank account. Log in. Spend two seconds looking at your balances. Log out. You will know where you stand that quickly. Think of your cash flow as waves rolling onto the beach. If the cash wave is big, you will notice and take action (this is when looking at the reports with the guidance of a pro is helpful). When the waves are small, you will surely notice that, too. Most of the time, I expect the cash waves will be normal, and no action will be required. But no matter what, you will always know. Because you will continue to do what you normally do: log into your bank account.

BUT IF I SET ASIDE MY PROFITS, HOW WILL I GROW?

This is a question I get asked a lot. By now I hope I've convinced you that chasing growth for its own sake is how you wind up broke and out of business. But that doesn't mean growth doesn't matter, or that you shouldn't want it.

Growth strategies have been part of my spiel for years. I have now written multiple books on the idea of fast, organic growth (like my book *Surge*). But like most entrepreneurs, I always used to think it was one or the other. Either you could grow or you could be profitable – you surely couldn't do both. I was wrong.

What I've found is that the fastest, healthiest growth comes from businesses that prioritize profit. And it is not because they plow money back into their businesses. Businesses that plow back their profits aren't truly profitable; they are just holding money temporarily (feigning profit), then spending it, just like any other expense.

Profit First sparks faster growth because it makes you reverse engineer your profitability. When you take your profit first, your business will tell you immediately whether it can afford the expenses you are incurring; it will tell you whether you are streamlined enough; it will tell you whether you have the right margins. If you find that you can't pay your bills after taking your profit first, you must address all those points and make the fixes.

Taking profit first will help you figure out which of the many things you do makes money, and which don't. Then the direction is obvious – you do more of what is profitable, and you fix (or dump) what is not. You will focus on what makes profit for you, naturally, and you will get better and better at it. And when you get better at what your customers already want and like, they will like you more. All this translates into fast, healthy growth. Boom!

Specialists, such as heart surgeons, know the secret. Keep doing a few things (like heart surgery) really, really well, and you will attract the best customers, dictate the biggest premiums, and see

25

your practice grow to be world renowned. Alternatively, the general practitioner does everything (from hangnails to rashes, coughs, and colds), but never specializes and therefore attracts the general customers. And when things get serious for the patient – that cough is actually indicating heart disease – the general practitioner refers the work to the specialist (who then collects all the premium money for her services). Specialists own the biggest houses in town, while general practitioners can't pay off their student loans.

To grow the biggest and the fastest, you need to be the best at one thing you do. And to become the best at something, you need to first determine what you are best at and do it a whole lot better. To get there, you take your profit first and the answers to being the best at something will reveal themselves.

THE NEW ACCOUNTING FORMULA

Now you know the psychology behind how you work. The next step is to put a system around the normal you. And we start with a simple new Profit First formula:

Sales – Profit = Expenses

What you are about to learn isn't anything new (not even to you). It is something I suspect you have been aware of – in full or at least in part – but have never done. It is the concept of 'pay yourself first' meets 'small plate servings' meets 'Grandma's envelope-money management system' meets your pre-existing natural, human tendencies.

Here's how you apply the four principles:

1. **Use small plates:** When money comes into your main INCOME account, it simply acts as a serving tray for the other accounts. You then periodically disperse all the money from the INCOME account into different accounts in predetermined

percentages. Each of these accounts has a different objective: one is for profit, one for owner's compensation, another for taxes, and another for operating expenses. Collectively, these are the five foundational accounts (Income, Profit, Owner's Comp, Tax, and Operating Expenses), and where you should get started, but advanced users will use additional accounts.

2. **Serve sequentially:** Always, always allocate money based upon the percentages to the accounts first. Never, ever, ever pay bills first. The money moves from the INCOME account to your PROFIT account, OWNER'S COMP, TAX, and OPEX (OPERATING EXPENSES). Then you pay bills only with what is available in the OPEX account. No exceptions. And if there isn't enough money left for expenses? This does not mean you need to pull from the other accounts. What it does mean is that your business is telling you that you can't afford those expenses and need to get rid of them. Eliminating unnecessary expenses will bring more health to your business than you can ever imagine.

3. **Remove temptation:** Move your PROFIT account and other 'tempting' accounts out of arm's reach. Make it really hard and painful to get to that money, thereby removing the temptation to 'borrow' (i.e., steal) from yourself. Use an accountability mechanism to prevent access, except for the right reason.

4. **Enforce a rhythm:** Do your allocations and payables twice a month (specifically, on the tenth and twenty-fifth). Don't pay only when there is money piled up in the account. Get into a rhythm of allocating your income, and paying bills twice a month so that you can see how cash accumulates and where the money really goes. This is controlled recurring and frequent cash flow management, not by-the-seat-of-your pants cash management.

By the time I started applying this small plate philosophy to my company's finances, I was doing consulting work and speaking on entrepreneurship. I also applied my new Profit First system to my one surviving investment, Hedgehog Leatherworks. I had given up booze and infomercials as coping mechanisms, and my depression had lifted. At the time, I was putting the finishing touches on my first business book, *The Toilet Paper Entrepreneur*, into which I inserted a small section about the concept of Profit First. After the book came out, I continued to refine the system, exploring and living it, and everything changed. I started implementing it with other entrepreneurs. And it worked – for me, for them, and for my readers.

Fueled by my passion for entrepreneurship and my determination to be profitable now, not at some indeterminate date in the future, I set about to perfect my system. In that process I discovered other entrepreneurs and business leaders who were running their businesses check to check and desperately needed the Profit First system. But I also found entrepreneurs and business leaders who had been implementing a similar system with great success. People like Jesse Cole, owner of two AAA baseball teams, who, while growing his businesses, paid off nearly $1 million in loans. And Phil Tirone, who, while building his first, highly profitable multimillion dollar business, continued to rent the same studio apartment until he determined that he had secured enough profit to upgrade – to a one bedroom.

In the coming chapters I will explain the way in which we tailor Profit First for Profit First for Tradies.

GET STARTED...

Tick all the boxes on pages 15 and 16 that apply to you.

Chapter 2

SETTING UP YOUR PROFIT FIRST BANK ACCOUNTS

SETTING UP YOUR ACCOUNTS

When Steve, an electrician, came on board as a Profit First client he was determined he didn't need to set up 'all those bloody bank accounts' because he 'didn't have the time'. Steve felt that as he already had three bank accounts he had been using, he didn't need anything else. Steve had his main account which had his invoices paid into and his expenses going out of, and he wanted to keep this as is. He had an account for putting away GST 'when he could afford to', and his third account had a zero balance but was set up with the intention of using it to put money aside for his staff pays, tax and super so he wasn't short when these were due.

I explained to Steve that setting up the seven foundational bank accounts is a vital step in the Profit First method, and using the seven foundational bank accounts actually makes it easier to follow Profit First. But Steve chose to stick to his guns and stay with his three bank accounts. We implemented Profit First in his business with Steve only using his three accounts.

About four weeks later I got a phone call from Steve which went something along the lines of: 'I'm ready to do Profit First properly now; I've opened all the bank accounts as you recommended at the start.'

What was even more exciting was the email I received the next week after Steve had done his weekly allocations using the seven bank accounts.

> Hi Katie
>
> I feel much better being able to see my money in each of the bank accounts and know what each is for at a quick glance. No more calculating what amount is for what now. It makes it much easier to wrap my head around Profit First now I am doing it right. Sorry for being a pain at the start.
>
> Steve

My suggestion to Steve and anyone who is implementing Profit First is to look for a bank with no monthly account fees. You don't want to waste your hard-earned money on bank fees. There are a number of banks now that offer fee-free monthly accounts. I use NAB for my seven foundational accounts, and BankWest for my 'out of sight, out of mind' accounts (more on these later). You can download a printable list from the Tool Box section at www.profitfirstfortradies.com.au/toolkit.

Setting up your bank accounts can feel like a big step for some, and for others this is an exciting time as you are finally getting started with Profit First. Remember, this is just like setting up your envelopes that our grandparents would have used or setting up our small plates if we are working on eating healthily.

There's no time like the present. Stop reading and start setting up your bank accounts. Do not wait any longer and do not be put off by the thought of dealing with your bank. I know dealing with banks can be a little painful, but now is the time to rip the Band-Aid off and just get it done. You only have to do this part once, and then not only is it done but you will be one step closer to getting Profit First set up in your business.

Don't wait for later as we all know later never comes. Getting this step done helps you build your financial foundation, and for it to be rock solid you need to open the bank accounts, all of the bank accounts. Only opening some of these accounts would be the equivalent to only putting in half the piers on a new house slab. Once the house is built it might stand for a little while before it gets rocky and eventually falls down. Put in the time now – it will mean success for you in the future.

Profit First for Tradies has seven foundational bank accounts. They are:

1. Income

2. GST

3. Materials and Subcontractors

4. Profit

5. Owner's Comp

6. Tax

7. Opex

These accounts need to be set up as regular bank accounts which can accept both deposits and withdrawals. Each bank is different, but in many cases online savings accounts can't easily accept deposits and withdrawals. So, please check with your bank before opening online savings accounts.

If you are staying with your current bank then you may be able to open new accounts through your online banking without even having to speak to anyone. If you are choosing a new bank that you have not dealt with before then you will need to complete your ID check – this usually involves visiting a branch, although for some banks you can be identified at your post office. Either way, get it done ASAP so you can get started.

Keep in mind that you do not need a card on any of these accounts except your Opex account, as that will be the only bank account you will be paying bills out of.

Once your accounts are set up, in your internet banking you can rename them to coincide with the seven foundational bank accounts to make it easier for you to see which account is for what purpose.

There are two other bank accounts that you need to complete the basic Profit First set up. These are accounts which should be 'out of sight, out of mind' as you want to park your funds here for a longer period of time and not see them every day. Your profit account and your taxes account (in addition to the profit and taxes account you have at your first bank) are for you to transfer your profit and taxes funds into so the balances don't flash before your eyes every time you log into your internet banking.

The way we behave as humans tells us that if this money is in our regular accounts for us to see each and every day, we are more likely to 'borrow' from those accounts, and 'borrowing' money from areas of the business that already have a purpose is what gets tradies into trouble. If it is harder for us to see and reach then we are less likely to stay in the habit of borrowing from those accounts. Borrowing money that is to be used to pay their taxes is the number one issue I see with my tradie clients. Cash flow is tight, so they borrow from those tax savings with the intention of topping up the tax account again before the tax bill is due. But when the tax bill comes in, cash flow has still been tight and the money isn't there, which usually results in a payment plan with the ATO, and you have just gotten on the treadmill with the ATO which unless you turn your cash flow around is very difficult to get off.

Once you have your bank accounts set up, you can see very clearly what cash you have for what purpose, which means you can make decisions more easily.

WHY THE ADDITIONAL ACCOUNTS?

The five foundational bank accounts Mike discusses in *Profit First* form the basis of Profit First for Tradies. I add two bank accounts to this foundation: GST and Materials and Subcontractors, taking the total foundational bank accounts for Profit First for Tradies to seven.

The biggest debt of 90% of the tradies I see is their debt with the ATO, and often the majority of this debt is from tradies collecting GST and then using it to help their cash flow. The problem arises when the business activity statement (BAS) is due and the cash is not there. One of two things happens:

1. The tradie ignores the BAS due date and hopes to get caught up and pay before the ATO comes knocking.

2. The tradie works even more hours to try to 'catch up', which just adds to the cycle of working crazy hours and leads to more stress and burnout.

By adding a GST account to the five foundational accounts you start the habit of putting GST aside first, before anything else, because it is not your money – you are simple holding it for the quarter until you are due to give it to the ATO.

Visit www.profitfirstfortradies.com.au/toolkit to download your visual copy of how this looks when set up.

TWO 'NO-TEMPTATION' ACCOUNTS

Now that you've set up your foundational accounts at your primary bank, your next step is to set up two 'no-temptation' accounts. We are going to get your taxes out of sight and out of mind. And we are going to do the same with your PROFIT account.

You may be thinking, 'Why do I need to do this? I already have a TAX account and PROFIT account at my primary bank. Why do I need a duplicate?' The reason we have these secondary accounts is to keep the money that you allocate and reserve for tax and profit out of your sight. Because when something isn't available to consume, you don't consume it.

If something is not readily available, we are unlikely to go through an extraordinary measure to consume it. Your profit is for you, and if you can access it easily, you might be tempted to 'borrow' from it to cover expenses. And the tax money? That belongs to the government. We are going to make sure you never borrow (a soft term for 'steal') from these accounts.

If you take money from your PROFIT account and put it back into the business, you are basically saying that you are unwilling to find a way to run your business with the operating expenses you allocated for it. If you take money from your TAX account, the money you have reserved to pay the government, you are stealing from the government. And I suspect you already know this, the government doesn't like that too much.

Find a new bank that you have never worked with before. In this case, you will not be moving money too much, and you will rarely bring the two accounts to a zero balance (unless you are short on tax). So with this bank, you can be less concerned about any minimum balance fees they have. At the second bank set up two savings accounts (this is where you will collect interest because your money will pool for a while). The two accounts are PROFIT HOLD and TAX HOLD. Then link these two accounts to the respective PROFIT and TAX accounts at your primary bank so that you are able to transfer money.

I will explain shortly when to transfer money and how often you will do it. But for now, I want to address one question you may have. You may be thinking, 'Why should I set up PROFIT and TAX accounts at both my primary bank and my no-temptation bank? I'm an entrepreneur! I like shortcuts! Can't I just transfer money from my primary bank's INCOME account to the PROFIT HOLD and TAX HOLD accounts at my no-temptation bank?' While technically speaking you can do that, it is a bad idea for two reasons.

1. Transfers from one bank to another are not instantaneous. It can take three days or longer (weekends and holidays add time), and when you log into your primary account, the money looks as if it is still there.

2. The goal with Profit First is to give you instant and accurate knowledge on where your cash stands. When you move money from one account to another at the same bank, the transfer usually happens instantaneously. By first moving money from your INCOME account to the PROFIT and TAX accounts (along with the other accounts), you will instantly see where your money stands, on their respective plates. Now that your money is clearly on the right 'plate' at your primary bank, initiate the transfer to the PROFIT HOLD and TAX HOLD accounts at the second bank. Now, anytime you log into your primary bank you will know exactly where you stand, even if the transfer to your no-temptation bank hasn't completed yet.

I also suggest you open these accounts at a different bank so that these funds you are holding for the future are not tempting you when you see them when you log on to your internet banking. We have all heard the saying 'out of sight, out of mind', and taking the time to open up two bank accounts at a different bank will play a large role in the success of Profit First in your business.

Remember, Profit First is about working with how we behave as humans and making sure we set up the system to make it easier for us in the long run. Yes, there may be some time you need to find to open these accounts, as if you haven't banked with them before you will need to do your 100-point identity check, but in the long run this small amount of pain will be far outweighed by the benefit of these accounts.

GET STARTED...

Step 1: Set up the seven foundational accounts:

1. INCOME account

2. GST account

3. MATERIALS AND SUBCONTRACTORS account

4. PROFIT account

5. OWNER'S COMP account

6. TAX account

7. OPEX account

You will already have a bank account or two open with your bank; as long as you aren't paying monthly account-keeping fees, keep your main account you already have as your OPEX Account. Then set up the remaining accounts:

1. INCOME account

2. GST account

3. MATERIALS AND SUBCONTRACTORS account

4. PROFIT account

5. OWNER'S COMP account

6. TAX account

Step 2: Set up two more accounts with another bank; remember, not the bank your other accounts are with.

1. PROFIT

2. TAX

Chapter 3

YOUR ALLOCATED PERCENTAGES

REAL REVENUE

Within Profit First we talk about 'real revenue', and the real revenue is what we use and base your percentage allocations on. Real revenue is your gross income less GST less your materials and subcontractors, as for tradies your materials and subcontractors would be greater than 20% of your gross income.

To successfully implement Profit First in your business you need to assess where your business is now. You need to assess your business so that you have a starting point to work from. I won't sugar-coat it, this can be a tough step, but one I guarantee when you put the effort in and do it correctly will pay you back tenfold.

There are three options when it comes to assessing your business from a Profit First view:

1. **Instant assessment:** which you can do yourself and then continue to work on Profit First yourself.

2. **Preparing for Profit First:** you can do this yourself or you can work with me to support you through this Profit First journey.

3. **Profit Assessment:** this is a one-on-one session with me to do a full Profit Assessment on your business. We then have a full report which we use as the basis to map out your Profit First implementation journey.

1. INSTANT ASSESSMENT

The instant assessment is a snapshot in time of your business and is an assessment you can do on your own. Keep in mind, for this to be correct you need to be looking at the right numbers in your business, which means your bookkeeping needs to be up to date. (In part III of this book I step you through how to review your bookkeeping.)

Keep in mind that Profit First is a cash-management system. There are two questions you need to ask yourself:

1. Did you get the cash or not?

2. Have you spent the cash or not?

It is that simple. Don't overcomplicate it with bookkeeping or tax talk like, 'I report on a cash basis or accrual basis', or, 'Do I include the money now I will get from ABC Company – they said they will pay this invoice on Friday?'

In Profit First we are always talking about cash that you have at that point in time when you are doing the assessment.

So that you can start your instant assessment, you will need:

1. Your profit and loss from your last full year in business.

2. Your balance sheet for the same year.

3. Tax returns for each owner in the business for the same tax period.

For those using Xero or similar software, you can get the reports mentioned at 1 and 2 easily.

Following is the Profit First Instant Assessment which you can complete now. For full instructions on how to do this and to download a printable copy, go to www.profitfirstfortradies.com.au/ toolkit.

	ACTUAL	TAP	PF$	DELTA	FIX
Top line revenue	A1				
GST	A2				
Material and subs	A3				
Real revenue	A4	100%	C4		
Profit	A5	B5	C5	D5	E5
Owner's comp	A6	B6	C6	D6	E6
Tax	A7	B7	C7	D7	E7
Operating expenses	A8	B8	C8	D8	E8

2. PREPARING FOR PROFIT FIRST

While the Instant Assessment has its place in the Profit First framework, as businesses in Australia are different to businesses in the US due to different laws and tax regulations, you may like to use the Preparing for Profit First worksheet instead. You can find this at www.profitfirstfortradies.com.au/toolkit.

This worksheet will step you through a series of questions about your business as well as your business and personal goals. Once you have completed that step, you then move onto the calculator which will help show you where your business is now, your current position, the goal, and then most importantly it will show you the gap.

The worksheet will also give you an easy list where you can review your business expenses as well as a section which will help you review your current pricing to make sure you are charging not only what you are worth but also that you are covering your expenses and allowing for a profit.[2]

So that you can gauge where your business is now, I suggest you stop reading, visit www.profitfirstfortradies.com.au/toolkit and complete the Preparing for Profit First worksheet on your business now.

3. THE PROFIT ASSESSMENT

If you are ready to jump into Profit First for Tradies then I recommend a full profit assessment, as this is a more thorough review of your business than the Preparing for Profit First worksheet. Nick, a brickie client of ours, reached out to us as he wanted to work with a certified Profit First Professional to help him with Profit First. Nick contacted us after reading Mike's *Profit First* and doing the Instant Assessment. He wasn't confident he had done it right and wanted to make sure that he was on track.

After our initial chat with Nick and discussing the Preparing for Profit First worksheet, he decided to do a full Profit Assessment session with us here at Profit First for Tradies as he had already decided he couldn't keep working the way he was. Nick was working 60-plus hours laying bricks each week and just couldn't get

---

2   This Preparing for Profit First worksheet can be completed yourself or I can work with you on this.

ahead. He also knew his body wouldn't be able to handle the hands-on work forever, and he had decided something had to change, so he sought out our help to work through a full Profit Assessment with him.

During the Profit Assessment we reviewed Nick's working and financial history of his business. We did find his bookkeeping needed a helping hand, so we paused the Profit Assessment to get the bookkeeping sorted out. As soon as that was done, we picked up the Profit Assessment but this time with figures that were correct and current for Nick's business.

Once we had a baseline of the historical numbers of Nick's business we then reviewed the following:

1. Nick's profit and loss, balance sheet and other figures to see if there were any trends in his numbers. Like most tradies, Nick's income and cash flow dries up around Christmas, and in some cases doesn't kick back in again till February and sometimes March. (This is a common problem I see with tradies and is something we work towards solving when we work one on one in our coaching program.)

2. We then reviewed Nick's profitability for the last two years of financial information.

3. We then categorised the historical Profit, Owner Payments, Tax, and Operating Expense percentages.

4. We then determined the CAPs (Current Allocated Percentages).

5. We then determined the TAPs (Target Allocated Percentages).

6. We then determined the transition from Nick's CAPs towards his TAPs over four to eight quarters.

7. We then analysed his current financial and business situation to identify areas to be addressed.

8. We had a one-on-one Zoom session with him to discuss his assessment and prepare for the next stage of his Profit First journey.

Once you have established where your business is today by completing one of the three suggested assessments above, we can then move on to working out what your targets are.

TWO COMMON PROBLEMS

Before we dig in, I want to address two common problems entrepreneurs face when they decide to start following the Profit First system – and they do not go hand in hand.

1. **Don't get bogged down in the details:** First, some entrepreneurs make the mistake of getting trapped in the details, spending hours, days, weeks or longer perfecting their percentages before they do anything. Worse, some entrepreneurs who get stuck in the minutiae never get around to doing anything. It's our old nemesis: analysis paralysis. In this chapter, we get down to the nitty-gritty, but if at any time you think you are lost in a research- and percentage-tweaking rabbit hole, stop and move on to the next chapter. Perfectionism kills every dream – better to just start.

2. **Look before you leap:** On the other hand, if you're like me, you might make the common mistake of taking action too big and too fast. I'm the type who starts before I have all of the information because most of the learning occurs in the doing anyway. But I put success at risk when I go into a situation ill prepared. In those cases, my ego blames the system when

mistakes were simply due to the fact that I didn't put in the necessary preparation.

I've seen entrepreneurs kick-start their Profit First system by taking a profit percentage of 20% immediately. They say, 'This is so simple. I get it. Bammo! Twenty percent! I'm done. Next problem.' Not so fast, chiefy. This is a classic mistake – one I've made myself.

Going full throttle into Profit First on the first day is like donating five gallons of blood at your first blood drive. You know what would happen if you tried to do that? You would die. The body has less than two gallons of blood pumping through it, so you'd keel over way before you reached your five-gallon goal anyway. However, there is a way to reach your goal in a safe way. If we donate small amounts over time, eventually we will donate five gallons – cumulatively. The Target Allocations Percentages, which we call TAPs, are simply the targets you are moving toward. To be clear, TAPs are not – I repeat, are *not* – your starting point. I derived the TAPs from surveys and evaluations of approximately one thousand of the most fiscally elite companies, across all industries and of all sizes, as well as an analysis of some of the thousands of companies who have implemented Profit First and, as a result, joined the fiscally elite. Aspire to move toward the TAPs. At this point, you may be thinking, "Mike, you don't know my industry. I could never hit those numbers." This is when I have to bring out the big guns, people like Henry Ford, who said, 'If you think you can or think you can't, you're right.' Be optimistic when you assume profit capabilities for your business or your industry. In other words, think you can. Your business may currently have higher numbers than the TAPs. If that's you, congratulations! This does not mean you can slow things down, however. You still need to push yourself. Try to become the elite of the elite.

CURRENT ALLOCATED PERCENTAGES

Your current allocated percentages are your starting point. Once you have completed your assessment you will have an understanding of your current allocated percentages. These may not look pretty but remember this is just your starting point. If your results from your assessment don't look great just remember it also means there is plenty of room for progress which means there are plenty of opportunities waiting to be uncovered in your business.

The main goals of Profit First for Tradies are for your business to make a profit that you actually get to keep and for you to pay yourself the wages you deserve.

For many of you, your Profit CAP will be 0 or even negative. Don't feel ashamed, upset or stressed about that. We can't go back and change the past; what we can do now you have learned more about Profit First is change your future profit. When you follow the Profit First method you will see your profit in your business rising as you implement Profit First and as your business gets financially stronger. While you may not have been paying attention to your profit in your business before, start small with 1% and work your way up.

You should also be paying yourself what the market cost would be to replace you if you were to hire someone to do your job. Now, I've worked with enough tradies over the years to know most of you are not taking a regular wage, let alone the one you deserve. This is about to change. Now, like anything, it won't happen overnight, but when we implement Profit First in your business your primary goal should be to pay yourself what you deserve.

To work out what your Owner's Comp CAP is, I'd like you to write down what your current wages are right now. I don't need you to look it up in Xero or refer to your tax returns. I just want you to write down the figure you have in your head for how much it is that you take from the business for 'wages' each year. Scribble it down here on this page if you need to; don't overthink it. In part II, Plan, I will give you step-by-step guidelines on how to thoroughly review your 'wages' as it is important that we know what we 'think' our wages are and what they 'actually' are. We need to make sure we get this number right as this is the target for our Owner's Comp %.

The quickest way to start taking a profit and the wages you deserve is to face your tax situation. The number one debt I see with tradies is debt to the ATO for past taxes not paid. I would say 75% of my clients come to me with a tax debt that feels so overwhelming they just don't feel like they will ever get out of it. What tends to happen is they ignore the fact they need to do their taxes until the last minute, which just compounds the problem, as the further behind you are the larger the tax problem feels. By tackling your tax early in your Profit First journey you will be able to get back on track. It is important to make sure you have a great tax accountant who can help you get your tax up to date and if necessary organise a repayment plan with the ATO. This repayment plan will be an expense from your Opex account, so the sooner you can get this paid off the healthier your Opex percentage will look. Each quarter you can use 99% of your Profit Account to put towards this debt if you so choose. The remaining 1% must be kept for you to spend on yourself as a reward for taking the risk of being the business owner.

TARGET ALLOCATED PERCENTAGES

Now you have worked out your real revenue range and the CAPs you fit into, you can get started on working out your allocations. Your target allocated percentages (TAPs) are just that, a target. This is where you aim to be; it is not what you start with. If you try to start at your TAPs you will have huge headaches, like Andy my landscaping client did. Prior to working with us, Andy had read *Profit First* and set the system up himself.

Andy fit into the real revenue range of B $250,000 to $500,000, so his Target Allocated Percentages are:[3]

	A	B	C	D	E	F
Real revenue range	$0–$250K	$250K–$500K	$500K–$1M	$1M–$5M	$5M–$10M	$10M–$50M
Real revenue	100%	100%	100%	100%	100%	100%
Profit	5%	5%	10%	15%	15%	20%
Owner's pay	50%	40%	30%	10%	5%	0
Tax*	15%	20%	20%	25%	25%	20%
Operating expenses	30%	35%	40%	50%	55%	60%

* We highly recommend that as a Profit First coach we collaborate with your tax accountant to ensure that your tax planning goals are reflected accurately in your Profit First percentages. Working with your tax accountant ensure that you have sufficient funds allocated to meet your full tax liability at the end of the financial year.

But Andy ran into trouble because he made two mistakes.

Firstly, he had been using his Tax account for GST, which sounds perfectly logical but was causing him headaches at BAS time as he had also put money aside for his company tax and his personal PAYG tax in this same account. As this Tax account balance was growing he had been tempted and dipped into it to buy some new tools, and after two BAS periods he realised he wouldn't have enough there for his company and personal PAYG tax come end of financial year.

The second mistake Andy made was he was using his TAPs for his allocations and was struggling to have enough money to pay his bills. Andy was confused as to why Profit First wasn't working for him.

---

3   This is the example for a company structure; please visit www.profitfirstfortradies.com.au/toolbox for examples of other structures.

How do you reach your goals?

This is the point where we face exactly where the business is – and it isn't always pretty. The upside is once we know exactly where a business is, it allows us to start making it better by setting up Profit First. This is the start of you being able to not only understand but take back control of your business, and the part where you can start learning to make better decisions now you have more knowledge.

I actually love this part of the Profit First process when working with clients like Andy. Even though I know this is the toughest part for my tradies, I also know that it's the point where it can start to be turned around. This is the point where it can all start to get better.

Now I'm the first to admit as someone who has worked in various roles in the financial industry my entire career and has run a successful bookkeeping business for some years now, I don't love profit and loss statements and balance sheets. Don't get me wrong; they absolutely have a purpose and are necessary in business, yet they are misunderstood and confusing to most business owners. They provide you the tradie with information on your business, but you often receive these after the fact and more often than not after many months have passed, which makes the information in those reports potentially no longer current.

This is one of the reasons why I love Profit First so much. When tradies implement Profit First they are taking control of their cash flow and are looking at their business in real time. In doing this they can make decisions much more quickly, which means they can fix any mistakes in their business sooner than months after the end of financial year (EOFY) when their tax accountant provides them with the profit and loss and balance sheet.

To get a snapshot of where your business is at the time we are working out your real revenue, TAPs and CAPs, we need to look at your profit and loss and balance sheet, and it's important that your bookkeeping is up to date and correct so that these reports are also correct. (I go into more detail in part III on how to make sure your bookkeeping is efficient and effective.)

GET STARTED...

Step 1: Tell those around you who matter that you are going to implement Profit First in your business. If they don't know what Profit First is, direct them to www.profitfirstfortradies.com.au/toolbox/WhatIs-ProfitFirst where they can watch a short video series which will explain to them what you are doing.

Step 2: Send your tax accountant and bookkeeper an email letting them know that you are implementing Profit First in your business. If they haven't heard about Profit First direct them to www.profitfirstfortradies.com.au/toolbox/WhatIsProfitFirst and let them know to watch the videos I specifically created for tax accountants and bookkeepers to explain what Profit First is and why they should get on board.[4]

Step 3: Set up your bank accounts if you haven't already done so. If you haven't already downloaded the bank account overview from the Profit First for Tradies toolbox do so now.

Step 4: Take the CAPs you worked out from page 44 and write them in the table below.

	TODAY	ADJUST	STARTING CAP
GST			
Materials and Subcontractors			
Profit			
Owner's comp			
Tax			
Opex			

---

4   If your tax accountant or bookkeeper is interested in becoming a certified Profit First Professional they can visit www.profitfirstaustralia.com.au 'Be a PFP' for more information.

Don't forget 10% for GST should be taken off your income first and placed in the GST account, then from what is left work out your allocated percentages.

Step 5: Make your first distribution. No time like the present. The very next time you have an invoice paid you are going to make your first allocation distributions. No excuses – let's get started.

Step 6: Celebrate. Congratulations; you have made massive changes to your business already. Setting up Profit First can feel really hard because it is new and different. Don't let that uncomfortable feeling that comes with change stop you from taking the steps to change your future.

Let's look at debt in the next chapter.

Chapter 4

FINDING FUNDS IN YOUR BUSINESS

UNCOVER THE MONEY THAT IS ALREADY IN YOUR BUSINESS

You have probably been with other tradies when everyone seems to be talking about their turnover and throwing large numbers around. Whenever a tradie talks turnover I get very, very nervous for them because in my experience it tells me they don't know their numbers and they are often not actually profitable at all. You see, turnover is just that: what the business income is for the year *without taking into consideration the expenses of the business.*

With Profit First we focus on the real revenue, as discussed earlier, to work out our percentages because we want to know the real numbers of our business. When we know our real revenue it allows us to focus not on the top line – turnover – but on the actual cash the business has.

When a business is thinking about and focused on turnover they also usually believe that increasing the turnover will result in an increase in profit, which it rarely does. In most cases, focusing on top line revenue and increasing sales without considering expenses is the best way to cause more stress and more debts. You see, in most instances increasing your top line also increases your expenses, and in many cases disproportionately, with a negative impact on your overall profit. Then you need to increase your income to cover the new increase in expenses, and the cycle continues until you are stressed and burnt out.

With all the tradies I have worked with on Profit First, we have always been able to find savings in their business without them missing out on things they need. Depending on how much of a situation your business is in there might be a tighter spending restriction than others have required.

Let's have a look at an example of uncovering some money that is already in your business.

Josh is a landscaper who had recently taken a hit financially when a large client of his folded and Josh's $25,000 invoice was not going to be paid. As you can imagine, this would be a major hit to any trades business, and was especially hard for Josh as he had recently become a new dad and was the sole income earner for his family.

Josh came to be a client of mine as he wasn't sure what to do next or how to recover from this loss, as he was already running pretty tight in the cash flow department.

When we started going through Josh's expenses he was lucky in the sense that he didn't have any debts in the business; he had recently finished paying off his lease on his ute and was up to date with the ATO – well, at least for the moment. He also had money aside for his upcoming BAS, but with this $25,000 no longer coming in he was thinking he would have to use those BAS funds to keep the business going and set up a payment arrangement with the ATO. But, he had done this in the past and it took him years to get out of the cycle of ATO payment arrangements, as he just couldn't get back on top of it. So, this is something he wanted to avoid if he could.

We also did the PRU process described above, and explained in detail on page 57, and were able to reduce his expenses by 12% without missing out on anything that Josh needed in the business. This not only allowed Josh to reduce his expenses while getting through this stage of his business, it gave him another increase in his profit as he was no longer spending money on these unnecessary expenses.

While Josh had made great progress in his expenses, it was still going to be a long journey to recover from this non-payment of the $25,000 invoice. 'I can take on more work to bring more money in,' Josh mentioned. We then reviewed Josh's workload and realised he did have some hours in the day and gaps in his week where he could fit more work in.

I also asked Josh when he had last increased his rates.

Josh paused, as I find happens with most of my clients. When the pause continued for longer than usual, I realised this was a sign that it had been a very long time since he'd reviewed his rates. As it turned out, Josh hadn't changed his rates since he started his business four years ago.

When I asked why, his response was, 'I've been too busy, and hadn't thought about it'. Again this is a very common response I hear from my tradies, no matter which trade they are in. It is uncomfortable for many of us, and I was the same in the early years of my business; we think it's better to get the job than not, so we often go in at a rate that we think is comfortable for the client. The problem is we get busy and forget to increase our rates, which then leads us to working long hours and not making the money we should be.

So, I suggested that Josh put his rates up by $30 an hour; he looked at me like I was crazy. 'I can't do that! No one will pay that,' was his reply. I suggested that Josh give it a try and see if he gets knocked back, and only after he gets three rejections would we review the rates again. Josh finished our meeting thinking I had lost my marbles, and I left the meeting excited to hear from Josh over the coming week.

A text from Josh arrived on the following Saturday apologising for bothering me on the weekend. Josh had sent out five quotes since we spoke last and increased his rate by $15 as he felt $30 was just too much. He'd had three of those quotes accepted and was yet to hear from the other two. 'Thanks for the push – I should have put it up more,' was the final line of the text.

With those three jobs at his increased rate he was all of a sudden much closer to increasing his income without increasing his costs. He would have done the same job with the same expenses at the old rate with a much smaller profit for the same amount of effort. Now, the part I really enjoy is once a tradie realises that the world will not end if they put up their rates, they become much more comfortable increasing them more right away. They keep testing their market with slight increases in rates until they receive three rejections that are purely because of price.

My suggestion to Josh was to choose a date or dates in the year and get into the rhythm of increasing his rate at these points in time. I always suggest that my tradies at least increase their rates the same as the Consumer Price Index each year as a bare minimum, otherwise they are going backwards.

I am not surprised when my tradies bump up their prices and their clients don't bat an eyelid. The tradies I work with are excellent craftspeople, and their clients appreciate the hard work they put into the job and are more than happy to pay them accordingly for their efforts. These are the clients you want to work with, not the clients who don't understand or appreciate your work, the ones who will always complain and will never be happy. Those clients you can leave for someone else; they are not the clients you want to attract, which is why I suggest that only after three rejections would we look at reducing the rate down as it allows for the odd painful potential client you may be quoting.

UNDERSTAND AND REDUCE DEBT

As we worked through his expenses and the list of debts was growing, not unusual for the tradies I work with, I could hear in Andy's
voice that the excitement of setting up Profit First in his business
was getting to the realisation stage. 'That debt is for the business so
it's okay?...Right?' Andy said, which is a pretty standard response
I hear when I work with my tradies.

The repayments on all your business debt don't show on your
profit and loss, but they do show on your balance sheet which
means it is not a true representation of the cash leaving your bank.
This is where business owners get into trouble as unfortunately
many business owners haven't been shown how to understand your
balance sheet to give you a true cash flow position. The balance
sheet will show all the outstanding debts your business owes, so
I understand why tradies don't always rush to look at this report as
it can be very overwhelming.

If you want to get more profitable in your business – and
remember, when I talk about profit I'm talking about actual profit
in the bank, not the paper profit found on your profit and loss statement – then you have to get honest about the debts in the business.
To do this, you need to make sure you look at the balance sheet and
look at all the debts, including leases, hire purchases, loans, money
owed to the ATO, and so on.

Now I understand this isn't a part of the book that excites.
I know exactly how this makes you feel because I too was in your
situation before I started using Profit First in my business. You do
not have to be embarrassed about the debt you have in your business. Just by reading this book you are doing more than most; you
are pulling your head out of the sand and starting to make changes
in your business to help you get out of this mess.

Congratulations.

The first thing that needs to be done is to freeze your debts; as
Mike talks about in *Profit First*, for now at least there is to be no new
debt taken on in the business. This isn't forever; once your business

is financially stable there are cases where getting new debt is okay and is useful to your business. For now though, put in place a debt freeze and let's get you out of debt.

Once you have frozen all your debts, the next step is to get rid of them. If you haven't read *The Barefoot Investor* by Scott Pape I highly recommend you do. Over the past few years Scott's book and his strategies have seen hundreds of thousands of average Aussies get out of debt and get their finances back on track. The 'domino your debts' strategy he suggests is the easiest to follow I have found, and is the one I used in my own business as well as what we used for our personal finances.

Scott's five simple steps for debt reduction are:

1. **Calculate:** List *all* your debts.

2. **Negotiate:** Contact your bank to see if you can negotiate a lower rate on your credit card and debts.

3. **Eliminate:** Cut up all your credit cards.

4. **Detonate:** List your debts from smallest to largest. Then, get rid of the smallest debt as quickly as possible by increasing the repayments.

5. **Celebrate:** When that smallest debt is paid in full, hold a bill-burning ceremony. The next day, keep your momentum and move on to knocking over your next debt domino. Keep going till you've paid them all off.

REVIEW EXPENSES

Once you have your debt organised and your debt reduction plan in place, it's time to review your expenses with the goal to reduce them by 10% below your current Opex to start with. Now, this isn't something most tradies can do overnight, and of course we don't want to cut expenses that will slow down or halt you earning an income; we want to make sure you are getting rid of those unwanted expenses that are eating away at your profit.

In *Profit First*, Mike suggests printing out 12 months of bank statements and taking the time to go through each transaction and mark it P, R or U, as follows:

P = Profit

R = Replace

U = Unnecessary

I do this with three different coloured highlighters; it doesn't matter which colour corresponds to P, R or U as long as they are clearly distinguishable from each other. Now I understand 12 months seems like a lot, but it is worth it. If 12 months is too much to begin with, start with three months: set aside some time and get stuck into it. Don't overthink it. You will find you have a number of recurring transactions each month which will make it quicker than you first think.

The next step is to cancel all the expenses which are U – unnecessary. This may mean you have to make a few phone calls to cancel some subscriptions or payments; once this is done you are saving your business money straight away. It might only be $10 a month, but I'm sure you would rather have $120 in your pocket at the end of the year than wasted on an unnecessary expense.

The next step is to review the 'replace' items to find a more cost-effective solution. Some of these will be able to be changed straight away; for example, insurance. You make a phone call and the policy is updated and the new amount starts. For others, such as phone contracts, you may have to wait if you are locked into a contract. I still recommend that you contact the company and ask anyway – you never know if you don't ask. If they say no, make sure you diarise the date in your calendar when that contract is up and call them then.

Now you are left with the expenses that make you profit. I suggest at this stage you look over this list again and make sure there isn't anything that could be moved to R (replace) or U (unnecessary), now you have had a chance to look over the other expenses. Then, with those that are left, again go through them and contact the supplier to get a better deal. You will be amazed at what you can get when you ask. Time and time again I have clients come back to me and say, 'I never thought XYZ company would give me a better deal than I already had, but they did'.

This process can be repeated each quarter, and I suggest you do. It becomes a much quicker process the more you do it, and it's well worth it every time.

GET STARTED...

Step 1: Review/increase your hourly rate.

Step 2: Implement a debt freeze.

Step 3: Start to domino your debts, paying off the smallest one first. Once that debt is eliminated, add the payment from that debt to the next one, and keep going – watch that snowball get bigger and bigger.

Step 4: Use 99% from your profit allocation each quarter to pay off your debt. The remaining 1% is for you to celebrate.[5]

Step 5: Review and reduce expenses by 10%.

---

5   For more information on eliminating your debts visit www.profitfirstfortradies.com.au/toolbox.

Chapter 5

EIGHT COMMON MISTAKES TO AVOID

As Mike writes in *Profit First*:

> The worst enemy of Profit First is not the economy, your staff, your customers, or your mother-in-law. (Well, it could be your mother-in-law.) The worst enemy of Profit First is you. The system is simple, but you have to have the discipline to implement it consistently, and that's where most of us fall short. We won't do the debt freeze all the way, or at all. We won't cut back on our staffing expenses or move into a grade-D office space. We surely won't challenge the industry norms and try to innovate. But we will steal from ourselves, taking money we originally allocated for profit to pay bills. We will steal from our TAX account to pay our own salaries. We'll borrow. We'll beg. We'll steal (from ourselves). And when we let Profit First fall apart, what is the single biggest reason why? We go it alone.

In chapter 11 of *Profit First* Mike lists his eight mistakes people make when implementing Profit First. Take note of these mistakes so that you can avoid falling into the same holes as others.

Mistake #1: Going it alone is the biggest mistake entrepreneurs make when implementing Profit First, but there are others.

Mistake #2: Too much too soon. It is extremely common for entrepreneurs new to Profit First to start putting 20% or even 30% into their PROFIT account right out of the gate. The next month they realize they can't afford it and pull the money back out to pay bills, which defeats the entire process. You must allocate profit and not touch it, so you've got to be sure that your business can handle the reduction in operating income.

To increase your profit, you need to become more efficient, to deliver the same or better results at a lower cost. Profit First works from the end goal backward. Once upon a time, you used to try to get more efficient in order to turn a profit. Now, by taking profit first, you must become efficient to support it. Same result, reverse engineered.

This is why I suggest you start with a small percentage. Don't fall into the trap of hogging all of the grub, taking too much profit up front and then shuffling most of it back into your OPERATING EXPENSES account when payroll comes due. Start with a small percentage to build the habit. Every quarter, move your Profit First allocation percentages closer to your goal by increasing them by an additional 1% or 2%. Starting slowly and moving slowly and deliberately will still force you to look for ways to get better and more efficient at what you do, but you won't be tempted to throw in the towel on the entire system because the pressure is too great or the task impossible.

Mistake #3: Grow first (and profit later). 'I like the idea of Profit First, but I want to grow my company.' This is probably the most common objection I get when I share Profit First with others. Too many entrepreneurs believe that you can have only one or the other: profit or growth. It sickens me that so many entrepreneurs think it is a trade-off. Pick growth or pick profit, but you can't have both. Bullshit! Profit and growth go hand in hand. The healthiest companies figure out how to consistently be profitable first and then do everything to grow that.

Maybe the lure of the four or five magical success stories we hear over and over again has caused this myth about profit and growth to take hold among entrepreneurs. You know, the stories about companies that skyrocket in growth, and after enough investors throw money at them, they turn a profit big time. I mean, don't you want to be the next Google or Facebook? If so, the path is clear: copy them. The problem with this strategy is the companies behind these same magical success stories are the lottery winners of the entrepreneurial game. They are not the rule, not even close. They are the one-in-a-million oddball successes, where the right approach was to grow, grow, grow and that sparked the turn to profit. Yet the 'grow at all costs' approach rarely results in profit. In fact, it is hard even to find stories you would recognize because the 'grow at all costs' mentality has produced a landscape of trashed, dumped, and destroyed businesses that you never heard of because no one ever talks about the failures (and that's another quirk of our behavior, called selection bias). But perhaps you are familiar with Twitter.

After ten years in business, Twitter still isn't profitable.[6] It has lost $2 billion since 2011, and has yet to figure out a way to make a penny in profit. It keeps hiring new management teams, new leadership, new anything to figure out a way to become profitable,

---

6   Twitter turned its first annual profit in 2018: https://investor.twitterinc.com/financial-information/financial-releases/default.aspx. A February 18, 2016, article titled 'Uber Says It Is Now Profitable in the US' by Dan Primack states that Uber states it is now profitable overall in the US, but that it is unclear how expenses are being allocated throughout Uber's global presence and therefore it is unclear when and/or how profitable Uber is. I suspect that if they used Profit First, it would be very clear...look at the profit account. http://money.cnn.com/2016/03/21/technology/twitter-10th-anniversary/.

but it can't. Isn't that crazy? To grow first and then try to figure out profit later? Twitter is trying to just that, and unless it pulls a miracle out of thin air, its well of investor capital is going to run dry. At the time of this printing, rumors have been circulating for years that the company is for sale, but it seems no one is interested. Maybe buyers are getting savvy and have decided that if a company can't figure out how to be profitable, they can't do it either.

The irony is that Twitter is just a massive example of what goes wrong when the focus is growth, leaving profit to be addressed in the future. This mentality is everywhere, and the scenario plays out in every size business. Grow at all costs. Until there is no money left and the end is a miserable lonely death. Fun times.

When profit comes first, your business will automatically show you the path to growth. I wonder how different Twitter would be had its founders committed to be profitable from day one? It would likely be a very different, and a much healthier company indeed.

Maybe the decree by Mark Cuban, the wildly successful entrepreneur and shark on *Shark Tank*, will set the record straight. In his February 2009 blog post titled 'The Mark Cuban Stimulus Plan,' he outlines what it takes for businesses to thrive and for him to invest money in their growth; my favourite bullets are 1. and 4.:

☐ '1. It can be an existing business or a start-up.'

☐ '4. It must be profitable within ninety days.'

I believe you need to be profitable starting today. One of the world's most famous investors gives leniency. He gives you the quarter.[7]

Mistake #4: Cutting the wrong costs. By now you know I'm a frugality junkie. I get a high from saving money, and I get the biggest rush when I find a way to eliminate an expense altogether. Still, not all expenses should be cut. We need to invest in assets, and I define assets as things that bring more efficiency to your business

---

7   Check out Cuban's entire investing strategy, as posted on his website at http://blogmaverick.com/2009/02/09/the-mark-cuban-stimulus-plan-open-source-funding/.

by allowing you to get more results at a lower cost per result. So if an expense makes it easier to get better results, keep it or purchase it.

I once toured the factory of a company that makes knives. When I noticed they were using old tools, one of the owners said, 'Yup. We even have systems from the 1960s! We save so much money by keeping our old equipment.'

During my tour, I also noticed that the knives they produced were inconsistent in terms of quality. Some of the knives were sharp; some were not. The handles rarely had a snug fit. Coincidentally, I had toured a different knife company earlier that week and noted that in one cumulative hour of manufacturing time they were able to turn out one perfect knife after another at a volume four times that of the company stuck in the decade of screaming Beatles fans and free love.

Money is made by efficiency – invest in it. If a purchase will bring up your bottom line and create significant efficiency, find ways to cut costs elsewhere, and consider different or discounted equipment (or resources, or services) rather than sacrifice efficiency for what you think are savings.

Mistake #5: 'Plowing back' and 'reinvesting'. We use fancy terms to justify taking money out of our different allocation accounts to cover expenses. Two that are used most often are plowback and reinvest, which are really just other ways to say borrow. I have done this. I 'plowed back' money from my PROFIT account to cover operating expenses, and boy, do I regret it.

When you don't have enough money in your OPEX account to cover expenses, it is a big red flag that your expenses are too high and you need to find a way to fix them fast. Once in a blue moon, it could also mean that you are allocating too much to Owner's Comp or Profit. This only happens when you start with a high Profit or Owner's Comp percentage. And when it happens, it is because you are taking a percentage of profit or pay that you are not yet able to sustain; the efficiencies are not yet in place to support your profitability. But again, this is rarely the reason your OPEX account is in the red.

Likewise, some entrepreneurs continue to use their credit cards for day-to-day operations and call them lines of credit. This is not accurate. It's money you don't have. Your credit card spending limit is almost never a bridge loan to carry the business for short cash flow gaps (e.g., a big profitable job isn't paying the bill on time as it was committed to). Nope. Credit cards are simply to use to pay expenses, resulting in debt, plain and simple. Using a credit card to cover what you can't afford is also a red flag that your expenses are too high. Stop using the credit card and reserve it for legitimate emergencies or unique circumstances (like for a purchase you must make to yield income).

When you find yourself in a situation where you feel the need to 'plow back' your profits, stop to reassess. There is always a better, more sustainable way to maintain the health of your business. You need to invest thought, not reinvest money.

Mistake #6: Raiding the tax account. In the first year or two of doing Profit First, you may get caught in a tax bind because you only pay your estimates. For example, your accountant may prepare estimates based on your business's prior year's income and profitability that say you should make payments of $5,000 every quarter.

As your PROFIT account and TAX account grow, you may be surprised to see that you're reserving about $8,000 in taxes each quarter. Seeing this, you might think, 'Hey, my accountant said I should pay $5,000 per quarter. I'm reserving too much for taxes.' A little voice inside your head may even say, 'Don't touch that money; you'll probably need it for taxes.' And then a louder voice will say, 'Nah, don't worry about it; you probably won't owe it and even if you do, you have time'. Cue the $3,000 withdrawal to pay yourself or pay bills. (A still louder voice – one I may have heard myself – might say: 'Why not start leasing a brand-new sports car with that money? Not only is it a business expense, you will instantly become the sexiest beast on this planet.' Do not listen! Danger, Will Robinson! Danger!)

Big mistake.

As your profitability grows, your taxes will, too. In fact, paying more taxes is an indicator that your business health is improving. Now, I am not saying you should ever pay more taxes than you need to (tax is just an expense like any other), but do realize that your taxes will grow as your business health does. So don't steal from your TAX account thinking you won't need that money for taxes. You will.

At times, you may even need more than you think. One year I messed up when I paid my estimated taxes every quarter and then used the extra money to increase my Owner's Comp when I discovered there was money left over. Dummy! Tax estimates are based on your prior year's income. If you make more profit this year (which you will), you will pay more taxes, but your tax estimates will not change. If you spend 'leftover' money from your TAX account simply because you allocate more than the estimate, you will be in shock come tax time.

Talk to an accountant who specializes in both profit maximization and tax minimization (if you are unsure whether they do, ask them to share their method[8]) every quarter to gauge how you are doing on taxes. And don't take money out of that TAX account! Your business is growing by leaps and bounds, and higher taxes are definitely in your future.

Another tax issue has to do with paying down debt. I call this paying for your sins because if you have debt you need to wipe out, implementing Profit First is going to hurt in the beginning. I should know – it happened to me.

Here's the problem: the government gives you a tax break on expenses but does not consider the money you reserve to pay down

---

8   I have created a list of Profit First Professionals who specialize in not just maximizing your profit, but also reducing your taxes. Choose the FIND option at http://ProfitFirst Professionals.com and we'll make an intro to an expert for you to consider.

debt an expense. The actual charges on your credit card and the interest and credit card fees can be expensed, but not your payments to pay down your cards.

I can't believe I'm saying this, but in this case, the government is right. You get the tax benefit in the year that you make the purchase – no matter if you paid for the expense in cash, by credit card or with funds from a bank loan or line of credit. As you become profitable and pay off debt, you will pay taxes on that income. Eliminating debt and paying taxes will feel like a double whammy. It isn't – you just need to pay for your 'sins.'

Mistake #7: Adding complexity. As Profit First grew in popularity, I found a completely unexpected failure point: people think it needs to be more complex. It is a weird phenomenon, but many entrepreneurs are so used to struggling with accounting details that they feel they need to struggle with Profit First. And if they are not struggling, they think something must be wrong. So they just make up rules to add confusion. I know this sounds odd, but I have seen it happen time and time again.

I have seen entrepreneurs modify their bank balances by introducing depreciation or amortization of stuff. Don't do this. Cash is cash. Either you have it or don't.

I have seen entrepreneurs take a profit distribution, put it in their savings, then pay for a purchase or make a hire with the money and say it is not an expense because it came out of their pocket. Ahhh! That is a shell game. And it is an expense. Profit is a reward (in the form of a cash distribution) for the equity owners of the business, and is above and beyond their pay from working in the business (Owner's Comp).

The system is super easy. It has been designed to work with how you naturally work; hence it is fluid. Don't overthink it. Don't add complexity. Don't try to 'outsmart' the system. Just get comfortable with the fact that sometimes getting the results you want is way easier to achieve than all the hard work you have put in to get the results you don't want.

Mistake #8: Skipping the bank accounts. Some folks try to 'simplify' Profit First by not setting up the bank accounts. They just have their bookkeeper manage it. They are entrepreneurs, after all, and don't have the time for 'unnecessary' nuances. So they use a spreadsheet or modify the chart of accounts in their accounting system to emulate the Profit First 'small plate' bank accounts. Then, immediately, Profit First fails to work. When this happens, they blame the system, but the problem is they didn't use the system.

Profit First must be set up to be directly in the path of the natural behavior of you, the entrepreneur. Because you log on to your bank account to look at your balance and make decisions, you must have Profit First there. Spreadsheets your accounting system's general ledger reports are also great, but they are also too late. You don't look at them when making in-the-moment money decisions; you look at them after the fact. Coming up with a battle plan after the battle is over is useless.

Profit First at the bank will be in your face every time you look at the accounts, enabling you to manage profitability and cash flow decisions in real time. Setting up your accounts means you can't avoid it, and that is exactly how it needs to be.

GET STARTED...

Step 1: Decide to commit to Profit First in your business.

Step 2: Remember to take Profit First one step at a time.

Step 3: Feel free to join Profit First for Tradies Facebook group.

Part II

PLAN

Chapter 6

SETTING GOALS

YOU'RE NOT ALONE

In Australia 80% of all small businesses fail within the first five years.

This statistic gets thrown around through the various media outlets often, and while it is not a very encouraging statistic, what I have found is that of those 20% who are 'lucky' enough to make it past the first five years, the majority of those are struggling more than they are admitting.

Struggling to pay bills on time.

Struggling to make payroll each week.

Struggling to keep up with their ATO commitments.

Struggling to take a wage for themselves.

Struggling to get people to pay them on time.

Struggling to hire great staff.

Struggling to maintain a work and personal life that they are happy with.

These are just some of the long list of issues many of those 'lucky' 20% who 'make it' past the five-year mark are facing.

The number one struggle I have found with every one of my tradies who has come to me – whether they have come to me for bookkeeping or for Profit First – has been their business cash flow has dried up, which has then dried up their personal cash flow. And more often than not they have reached a point where they have no room to borrow more to cover the shortfalls, which is only a temporary solution anyway. Often the bills are piling up, and there is usually a letter or two from the ATO that remains unopened because of the fear of what it will say and mean for the business.

The ability to borrow money via credit cards, personal loans, overdrafts, business loans and refinancing a home loan have long been seen as the answer to this problem. Borrow some money any way you can, and throw it back into the business. 'Get through this patch' and it will all be okay after next week/month/quarter/Easter/ Christmas … you get the idea.

Unfortunately, this plan rarely works long term as if nothing changes, nothing changes. If you stick to the same habits and processes that got you to this place, you will find yourself back in this same place, except this time with even more debt.

It's heartbreaking receiving a message like I did from Matt, a new concreting client of mine. The email arrived in the early hours of the morning (like they tend to):

'I've tried everything, I can't borrow any more money – what do I do?'

My heart sank when I sat at my computer that day and read Matt's email, as it does every time I get a message like this. I picked up the phone and called Matt immediately as I knew how he would be feeling. I have had quite a few of these types of messages over the years, and I know that once I talk to my clients they have some hope and can see that there are ways to help them get out of this vicious cycle that keeps them trapped in a silent hell.

During my conversation with Matt I assured him that his situation wasn't unique and he wasn't special; in fact, this is very common for tradies and a story I have heard time and time again.

'Really? I'm *not* the only one who let themselves get in this mess?' was Matt's response. Again, this is a response I have heard time and time again.

Tradies, like many business owners, have a terrible habit of not talking about the tough times they are going through in business. Yes, of course there is the odd comment between mates about working long hours, staff being painful at times and that cash flow could be better, but from my experience it stays at that level. The tradies I have worked with and helped over the years all thought they were the only ones who had these issues this bad. They thought they were the only ones who were 'failing'. They thought they were the only ones who couldn't get their act together.

I am here to tell you that you are not – you are part of the majority of tradies who are in business. Obviously that doesn't make it better, but it does help to know you are not the only one and you don't have to go through this alone.

To turn this around and to become part of the minority who are nailing their numbers, you do have to focus some of your energy on your numbers and you do have to do some work. I always tell my new clients that Profit First is a simple cash flow management system but at the start it's not always easy. The reason it is not easy isn't because of Profit First, it is because of us as humans: change can be difficult, and more difficult for some than others.

The upside of all this is that I have worked with a large number of tradies just like Matt who had the same worries and same stresses going on in their life and in their business. As Mike Michalowicz says, Profit First will 'transform your business from cash-eating monster to a money-making machine', and I was able to help them turn their businesses around using Profit First, even those who thought there was no hope.

I'm not going to sugar-coat it: it does take focus and commitment, like anything worth doing in life. I can't wave a magic wand like in the stories we read to our children and make it all perfect. We need to work together as a team to help you reach your Profit First goals. The purpose of this book is to give you a step-by-step guide to what you need to do, how you can do it, and why you need to do it, to make sure you successfully implement Profit First in your business.

Throughout this book you will find step-by-step instructions on how to set up Profit First for your trades business as well as real-life case studies of my clients who have graciously agreed to share their stories to help other tradies with their Profit First journey.

The most important step you need to take is to remember to ask for help before you waste your time struggling, whether it be a Profit First concept or just a question you have around how a particular area of Profit First will work in your business.[9]

SETTING YOUR GOALS

As I chatted to Matt about his concrete business it was clear that the life he thought he would have when he was self-employed compared the life he was currently living were worlds apart. While he was still technically able to pick and choose the jobs he took on, he felt as though he had to take on all the jobs otherwise people would stop sending work his way. The problem with this was that for many of these jobs he had priced them with very little margin so that he could get the work, with the plan that once the work consistently rolled in he would be able to increase his prices and would start making great money.

---

9   I want to hear from you. Don't be afraid to email me at katie@profitfirstfortradies.com.
au and use the subject: Profit First Help. I mean it; email me and I will reply to your
question. Make sure you give me 48 business hours to respond, but I would rather you
ask if you aren't sure than stress over it and it holds you back on your Profit First journey.

The jobs were now rolling in but a number of problems started to arise. Matt was now so busy he didn't have time to chat to those giving him the jobs to ask for an increase in price, nor did he feel very comfortable doing so. He was focused on getting the jobs done so he could get more work, and as the weeks turned into months (and months and months) and his cash flow was getting tighter and tighter, he began to wonder when he was going to have the freedom that other tradies seem to have.

After chatting further, we realised that Matt had never taken the time to sit down and really think about what he wanted out of his business. Matt, like many tradies, thought it would all fall into place – of course with the odd hiccup, but overall Matt thought being a self-employed tradie would give him the freedom to work shorter days or weeks if need be. He thought he would have the chance to take holidays when he wanted, but in reality he was working longer days and weeks than ever before, and the thought of taking a holiday filled him with dread rather than the excitement that it should.

Being self-employed comes with a number of challenges, many of which we will address in this book. To help us overcome those challenges we need to make sure firstly we have a really clear list of what we want out of our business, and then a map of how we are going to tick those goals off our list.

After working with numerous types of tradies over the last eight-plus years – from sole traders working on their own to companies with 15-plus staff plus a team of subbies, and everything in between – I have learnt that goal setting is not something that is high on their priority list. It certainly isn't something that makes their faces light up when I mention that we need to do it before we do anything else in their business. 'But can't we just sort out my bookkeeping?' and, 'Surely we can just get my cash flow under control without having to do this?' are two very common responses.

Once we get over the initial discomfort that occurs when I mention goal setting to my tradies, we dive into the good stuff: the reasons why you have taken the risk of going into business, and most importantly the rewards. The rewards are different for everyone. There are no rules: they are *your* rewards, and you can choose whatever you want them to be.

What rewards would you like for taking the risk that is being a business owner? Here's a table to get you thinking about this. I've included a few examples. You can draw up your own table, or you can write in the book if you prefer. You can also download and print a copy from www.profitfirstfortradies.com.au/toolkit.

I want more free time	I'd like more holidays
I want less stress	Able to buy more of what I want

You might like to come back to this and add things to your list as you think about them. This list should be your ultimate goals, without any thoughts about something not being possible. If there was nothing stopping you, what would your ultimate goals and rewards list include?

When thinking about your ultimate goals and rewards list, think about what you would like now first. What can you upgrade *now* which would make a difference to your and your family's life?

Would it include upgrading your car or your home? Would you like to sell and buy a larger house, or would you prefer to do an extension or renovation on your home? Maybe you would really like a motorbike or a ski boat?

Are your children at school and you would like to send them to a school that has better facilities than the average school? Do you have a child coming to the end of their schooling life and you would like to help them pay for a trip overseas once they finish? Or help them purchase their first car?

There are so many possibilities; many of these I have mentioned may not be on your list and that's fine. You can make your own list. There is no right or wrong; there is only what you would like.

Once you have listed the things you would like to change now, now start to think about some longer term goals and rewards you would like.

Have you always wanted a holiday home on the beach or at the snow? Would you like to take annual holidays to the beach, camping or to the mountains? Would you like to travel overseas every few years, or every year for that matter? Do you have a list of places you would like to travel to? If not, start one now. Or if travel is not your thing that is perfectly okay. If you have always wished you could buy a 1964 EH Holden and restore it to its original state or drop a nice 350 Chev in it, again whatever you want to put on your list, you can.

I often suggest to my tradies that they write this list and if they don't want to they can never show it to anyone, ever. This can be your private list. I know when I started doing this myself there were many things on my list I would never have shared with anyone, especially those close to me, for fear of feeling like they would laugh at me for my crazy dreams.

That is how you know you are writing the right list: when you think people may laugh or make a snide comment or two about what is on your list, you are listing all those dreams and goals that you deserve and are truly yours. Now, you might have great, supportive mates who are nothing but positive with whatever you say or do. Or you might have typical Aussie mates and family whose first reaction is to knock whatever it is you have said, even if they do it in jest. But it still can knock you back a little.

If you have been brave enough to share with others your goals and rewards list and they do make remarks which aren't the most positive, know that it actually doesn't matter if they think you can do what you say you can do or not. Obviously it would be great to have their support while you did these things, but it is even better to go ahead and do them and then have them compliment you on your achievements.

KEEPING IT SIMPLE

Now, I will confess goal setting was not my favourite thing to do in business for many, many years. I never felt comfortable writing out my 12-month plan, let alone a 3-, 5- or even a 10-year plan, as I didn't have the confidence that I would achieve any of it. I had no faith in my ability to reach the goals I was setting, so why bother setting them was my attitude. (I must say, a pretty poor attitude now I look back and am honest with myself.)

Why is setting goals and planning so important, and how did I overcome this?

Truthfully, I got sick and tired of being sick and tired. I was hating my business and nothing seemed to work. I had no direction and was just floundering around, which resulted in a not very happy me. I knew business would be hard; in fact, I swore black and blue I would never work for myself because I had seen how hard my family and friends around me had worked in their businesses and knew it wasn't for me. I didn't want to do business if it was going to be hard.

Yet here I was, in business. It was hard, stressful, and I had no goals that I committed to. I had goals and plans in my head, but that was it. Like so many tradies I work with, we have so much in our head and we still try to keep in there our goals and plans. But these get pushed to the back of our minds as we concentrate on other things like cash flow.

'Where focus goes, energy flows' is a Tony Robbins quote I had heard many times. So I took the advice of my mentor and wrote down my goals and plans for the next month, quarter, six months, twelve months, and three years to start with. Five and ten years seemed ridiculous at this stage, so I left those for the time being. Now, I love to plan parties and holidays, so I straight away went into detail mode and started to be really specific about how I was going to reach these goals. But then overwhelm kicked in pretty quickly, and I went back to my old thoughts of 'I'm never going to reach these'.

During the next session I had with my mentor, he was quick to point out that I needed to keep it short and sweet to start with. He instructed me to write a simple dot point plan:

- ☐ 1-month goal =

- ☐ Quarterly goal =

- ☐ 6-month goal =

- ☐ 12-month goal =

- ☐ 3-year goal =

He instructed me to think about what I wanted to achieve at the end of those times and write that down.

Keep it simple.

I followed his instructions, and I was done in a minute or two, allowing for a little amount of over-thinking time. I was amazed at how simple it could be, if I kept it simple.

I still use this with my coaching clients today. For each and every new client we take a couple of minutes at the beginning of our first session to find out what it is they want. What are their goals and plans? While this step can feel a little odd for some of my tradies, it is one thing I get thanked for having them do more often than not.

This simple step not only gives them time to think about what they actually want from their business and for their life, it also gives me insight into their hopes and dreams so I can customise their Profit First journey to help them reach their goals. This step helps me build their Profit First map and helps me make sure I create the most efficient route for them to take.

I find that many tradies have the same or similar goals. Many of them include:

☐ 1-month goal = Figure out where my money is going

☐ Quarterly goal = Pay the BAS on time

☐ 6-month goal = Get caught up with the bills

☐ 12-month goal = Take a holiday and have money to come back to

☐ 3-year goal = Get off the tools and be making a decent profit

Whether your goals are similar to those above or completely different, it doesn't matter. What is important is that you have goals that you make a conscious effort to work towards. Otherwise you will keep getting the same results, and if you aren't happy with those results then that isn't a very fun self-employed journey.

GET STARTED...

What are your business goals?

• 1-month goal =

• Quarterly goal =

• 6-month goal =

• 12-month goal =

• 3-year goal =

Keeping your goals simple gives you a much higher chance of making the changes you need to make to be able to start working towards reaching them. Once you have these goals written down you can start to work out the finer details and begin planning how you are going to make them happen.

The great news is that when you implement Profit First, most of these plans will happen and these goals become easy to achieve.

The response I usually receive after doing this is, 'Why didn't I do this sooner?', which is usually followed by a large sigh and sometimes a few choice words about themselves which I am not allowed to publish in this book. They, just like I did, kick themselves for not finding a specialist earlier to help with these issues in their business.

Once we tackle these fundamental goals with Profit First we can start focusing on the fun goals like a trip to watch Daniel Ricciardo race in the Formula 1 at Monaco, a weekend at Phillip Island to watch the Moto GP, or whatever it is you chose, all without worrying about how you are going to pay for it (hello profit account and regular income). With Profit First you will not only have money to do all these things you had dreamed about but you can also come back to a business which has still been earning an income while you are away, which means the days of a dip in income after you have had time off can be a distant memory.

GET STARTED...

So let's do the goals list again, but this time write down what your FUN goals are, and this time we are going to add in our 5- and 10-year goals:

- 1-month goal =
- Quarterly goal =
- 6-month goal =
- 12-month goal =
- 3-year goal =
- 5-year goal =
- 10-year goal =

Chapter 7

ASSESSING WHERE YOU ARE NOW

GETTING ON TRACK

My Profit First journey had a couple of false starts; actually, more than a couple if I'm being honest. I had every excuse under the sun as to why I couldn't do my percentages this week. I justified it to myself with the usual stories: 'I'll just miss this one', 'I'll catch up next time I get invoices paid', 'I just have to finish this one project'. I saw Profit First working wonders for other business owners around me and yet I came up with more excuses: 'They have a bigger business than I do', 'They have more [insert any excuse I could find here]'.

Habits are hard to break, and at one stage I thought Profit First wasn't for me so I plodded along with my business, doing what I had always done, and I kept getting the same outcome. No surprises there. The outcome wasn't what I had dreamed of, and it certainly wasn't what I wanted from my business. Yet here I was, exactly where I said I would never be. At this stage I hated my business and couldn't see how I could make it work.

To help me get out of this rut, my business coach, the same person who had introduced me to Profit First, asked me to do one simple task: go through my client list and highlight those I loved working with and see if there were any similarities. Well, there were; my highlighted list consisted of all my tradie clients. Tradies, the clients I had originally started out wanting to work with, had somehow become a mismatch of tradies and other business types that I didn't enjoy working with.

So, in an effort to get the business going where I wanted it to, I politely emailed all those who weren't in my desired market to let them know my business was taking a new direction and that I would only be working with tradies from that point. The business income took a huge hit, one I couldn't really afford at the time, but I knew I had to do it to get back to having a business I actually enjoyed.

After I did this simple task and with much less income coming in, I realised I had to change something else. I dug out my already well read *Profit First* book and read it again, this time vowing to implement it in my business 100% without any excuses.

The first thing I did was reach out to someone I knew who had much more Profit First experience than I had. I sought the advice of a specialist, Laura Elkaslassy, as she is a Profit First Professional. Laura also had a bookkeeping business before starting her Profit First coaching, so I knew she would be able to help point me in the right direction.

After chatting with Laura to clarify some questions I had – as we have a few differences such as GST compared to how Mike describes things in the book – my Profit First journey started (again). That one conversation turned my Profit First journey around as well as my business, and here I am today, writing *Profit First for Tradies*, which all started because of me reaching out to Laura, the specialist in Profit First.

There are two reasons for sharing my story with you. Firstly, everyone has bumps in the road when they are travelling through their business journey, even with the best map, and some of those bumps can feel like mountains that are unable to be crossed. Secondly, the key to making following that map easier is finding people who have successfully done what you want to do and getting them to help you. If I hadn't reached out to Laura, I know I would not be at the place I am today with my business. I would still be a struggling business owner working long hours trying to make ends meet.

For your business to be successful and for you to reach your ultimate goals, you need to have a look at where your business is now. You need to have a crystal clear idea of exactly where you are starting from to be able to draw a clear map to where you want to go. I'm not going to sugar-coat it: this can be a very hard part of the journey. I know it was for me in my business. I also know that if you don't take the time to be really honest at this stage then progress is slow as a result.

When we coach our tradie clients we help guide them through this stage of the financial map to make it as quick and pain free as possible. We rip the Band-Aid off quickly. We know once you get clear on where you are – and I mean where you *really* are, no matter how horrible it may look – we can then start taking the necessary steps to get you out of that dead end on your financial map and start heading towards the beautiful beach where relaxation and cocktails are waiting (if you are so inclined).

We take you through an assessment of your business, which lets us get clear on where your business is now. It is an assessment at a snapshot in time which highlights for us which areas of the business we need to focus on. It allows us to prioritise and plan your financial map into steps that are clear and simple. We look at your financials in detail, and require you to look at things such as your profit and loss and your balance sheet. In most cases we will look at some other reports too, depending on your business. It is vital that this information is correct and up to date – this information is the foundation of your Profit First journey and we need to make sure it is right.

In most cases, before working with a client on Profit First we take a step back and review their bookkeeping, or lack thereof for some, and make sure they are set up to be as efficient as possible. We make sure your foundation is solid and your bookkeeping becomes quick and easy. I know; quick and easy are not usually two words tradies would associate with bookkeeping, but I and my team have been working with tradies just like you for years. We have streamlined our processes so we can help you organise your bookkeeping in the least amount of time possible. (In part III we will dive into how we do this, and show you how much you will benefit from finally organising your bookkeeping once and for all.)

HOW MUCH DO YOU NEED TO LIVE ON?

As I mentioned in part I when discussing debt reduction, *The Barefoot Investor* by Scott Pape is a must read. He is the master of personal finances, and I again strongly recommend you purchase and read his book. It will transform your personal finances, which go hand in hand with your business finances.

Possibly the most important part of reviewing where you are now is working through the following four steps:

- ☐ **Step 1:** How much are you spending now?

- ☐ **Step 2:** How much are you actually spending?

- ☐ **Step 3:** How much can you afford to spend right now?

- ☐ **Step 4:** How will you live on your current owner's comp figure?

Let's have a look at each of these.

Step 1: How much are you spending now?

This part usually isn't much fun; you are not alone if you feel like skipping this section of the book. But those who don't skip this section and who do the exercises are the ones who are able to move their business to the next stage and are able to make their lives infinitely better as a result of sticking with this now. My suggestion is to just get it done.

There is a simple way to get started, and once you do, the hard part is done. After this, it is much easier to maintain.

Here's what you do.

Set 30 minutes aside and print out your personal bank statements for the past three months. You can do 12 months if you like, but I usually suggest three so you don't feel overwhelmed and give up. Grab a highlighter, pen or pencil and mark everything that is 'essential', and I mean *essential*. These would be things like:

☐ mortgage payments (so you have a roof over your head)

☐ rates (so you have a roof over your head)

☐ electricity (so you have the power to run your house)

☐ water (so you can have showers, wash clothes, cook and drink).

Then take a different colour and highlight your other expenses which are 'must haves', even if they are not actually 'essential' for you to survive. These would be things like:

☐ phone

☐ internet

☐ insurances such as car insurance, home and contents insurance, health insurance

☐ car registration

☐ groceries

- ☐ school fees
- ☐ kids' sports fees.

Take a third colour and highlight the 'nice to haves':

- ☐ subscription TV
- ☐ dinners out
- ☐ holidays
- ☐ weekends away.

Now keep in mind that apart from the essential list, everyone's must haves and nice to haves will be different. It is up to you what goes on which list. When I do this with clients I certainly do not go through the list with a red pen and cross out those things I believe are on the wrong list.

This is your choice; there is no right or wrong. This is about your priorities.

Once you have gone through your statements and highlighted them, you can then add up roughly what you have spent over that time for each category. Now, I say roughly because if you haven't reviewed your spending like this before, chances are you aren't over the moon to be doing so. So rough and done is better than not done at all.

Step 2: How much are you actually spending?

Now do the same with your business bank accounts; print out your bank statements for the past 12 months. Grab a highlighter, pen, pencil or whatever and mark every time you took money out of the business for personal expenses. You might have marked the trans-actions as wages or drawings, or you may have paid for personal items out of your business account. Highlight them all, and once you are done, add them all up.

Usually this amount is considerably higher than expected; that is normal for 99% of the tradies I work with.

This exercise will do two things for you; firstly, it will likely freak you out, but don't worry – we have steps to help you maintain your spending without missing out. And secondly, it will give you a reality check about what you actually take from the business so that we can implement strategies to help you be conscious of your spending habits.

Step 3: How much can you afford to spend right now?

In part I of the book we discussed your owner's comp based on your business real revenue; this figure may or may not be what you need to cover your personal expenses, which we have calculated in step 1 and step 2.

This figure gives you a starting point – your next figure will be what your business needs to make for you. Your owner's comp account will be where you withdraw your 'wages', which will be equal to this amount to start with. Your business will then also have to allow for tax and superannuation on this wage, which will stay in your owner's comp account until they fall due.

What is the difference between your owner's comp amount and the amounts you have calculated in step 1 and step 2 here?

Step 4: How will you live on your current owner's comp figure?

I first want to make it clear that like most tradies you will need to reduce your spending if step 1, 2 and 3 above have shown you are spending more than your business can sustain. Your past spending habits, if continued, will see you and your business struggle even more than you are now. In this book, my goal is to have you struggle less not more, and reducing your spending for a period of time can be temporary and it should be temporary. Your business should work for you – you shouldn't be a slave to your business. Knowing these figures is a great start on your journey towards building your business to support you and your financial goals.

So, how do we reduce your personal spending without doing without everything you want?

We do three things:

1. prioritise
2. plan
3. profit.

Step 1: Prioritise

Go through your lists you have created: essentials, must haves and nice to haves. Prioritise which expenses you will review first.

While going through all of them is great, that often doesn't happen as tradies either get overwhelmed and it causes them to not do anything at all or they don't make the time to do this as they don't think it will make much of a difference. So, I suggest highlighting your top three and working on those first, then once those are done, your next three, and so on until you have worked through them all. Once you have done this the first time, you will find this process becomes much quicker each time you do it. I suggest to all my tradies that they do this once per year at least.

Now, the essentials are non-negotiable and need to be paid for; we can all agree on that. But the issue with the essentials is, have you negotiated the best deal? For example, when was the last time you called your bank and asked for a reduction on your interest rate on your home loan?

Obviously you can't negotiate your rates with your council as they are set, but can you negotiate other services that are included on your rates notice? For example, in our council area they offer a reduction on your rates notice if you take a smaller bin as they are encouraging people to recycle more.

When was the last time you called your electricity company to make sure you are getting the best deal? You could also look at changing electricity companies to get a better deal. There are a number of options for you if you set aside 15 minutes and make a phone call or two.

Water rates are usually locked at a set rate, but could you look at taking shorter showers? Even just a couple of minutes a day over the course of three months will add up.

Most big changes come from a number of smaller changes that all add up. Don't expect to find one expense you can reduce dramatically and it will make everything alright. One dramatic change usually comes with an equal amount of discomfort. Look for those expenses that you can make small changes to which usually causes a smaller amount of discomfort, making these changes much easier to make and – more importantly – sustain.

Repeat this process with your must haves, and with your nice to haves.

Step 2: Plan

Once you have prioritised the order in which you will review your expenses to find those savings, make a plan on how you will do it.

For example, you might set aside an hour or two once a week until you have gone through everything. Or you might prefer to mark a full day in your calendar and get stuck into it all at once. How you plan to do it is up to you, you just need to make sure you make a plan and stick to it. I would suggest that you mark it in your calendar to help you get it done.

Step 3: Profit

For many it feels like a drag to go through all your personal expenses; I mean, you haven't done too bad by *not* doing this in the past, right? But my guess is, if you are reading this book, what you have done in the past is no longer cutting it and you need something to change. The sooner you do this, the sooner you will see the benefits and the sooner Profit First will start to make a difference in your business and your life.

These steps are something I go through with my clients to keep them on track and to get through it more quickly than they may have done if they were doing it by themselves. Accountability and support make all the difference in this step.

GET STARTED...

Step 1: Work out how much you need to live on by reviewing your current spending habits.

Step 2: Review and reduce your current spending habits by 10%.

Step 3: Compare your current income need to the owner's comp amount you calculated that your business can afford to pay you now. How much is the difference?

Chapter 8

BUILDING YOUR FINANCIAL TEAM

Being self-employed is a team sport, yet I see so many new clients trying to play it as an individual sport and they are failing. They are often working themselves into the ground, and have unhappy families because they rarely see them, and when they do they are either stuck 'doing paperwork' or they are so tired they can barely keep their eyes open.

If this is you, it's time to get some help.

THE PLAYERS

Now is the perfect time to build your financial team just the way you want it. Your core financial team should be made up of the following people:

☐ you

☐ your bookkeeper

☐   your tax accountant

☐   your Profit First Coach

Each of these people plays a vital and distinct role in the success of your business. If you don't have an accountant or bookkeeper who you feel is helping you make the most of your business, you need to find new people. Don't stay with them because you have been with them for years, or they were introduced to you by a mate or because you haven't had time to find a new one.

You should also have other specialists who help in your business for a particular project, and then once you have, for example, a particular program set up and they have provided training for you they will finish being part of your financial team.

So, how do you know if you have a great fit for your financial team?

You

The first person on your team, you, needs to make the decision that you are ready to learn and educate yourself on the financial side of your business. Do you need to be an expert? No, but you do need to have some knowledge, at least enough to know when something isn't right financially in your business and you are ready to tell your financial team you feel there is a problem. It is then their job to investigate and bring you a solution. Sometimes that solution is more education for you; other times it is them having to correct something.

Your bookkeeper

Your bookkeeper should always be up to date and using and suggesting technology and apps that make your business run efficiently. They should be using Xero or another online accounting system, and they should be recommending receipts programs such as Hub-Doc at the bare minimum to help make your bookkeeping efficient.

If they aren't expert in these and are not helping you use such tools, they are not who you need.

They need to have the capability to keep your bookkeeping up to date on at least a weekly basis, and to keep you up to date with what you owe and when payments are due. They should also have processes in place to ensure they follow up promptly if they need any information from you so that they can keep your bookkeeping up to date.

Your bookkeeper should also be able to recommend other apps or programs to capture other data, such as staff and subbies start and finish times and which jobs they are on, so that they can track back to the job how many hours are being used on that job. They should also know who to refer you to regarding a more robust quoting and job management program to use, again to easily capture more data on your jobs.

They should also have an excellent network of other financial professionals who you may need now or down the track, such as accountants, HR specialists, a mortgage broker and an insurance broker. They should be able to give you referrals to people they have worked with personally and know what level of service you are getting.

Your tax accountant

Your tax accountant, like your bookkeeper, should be up to date with technology and willing and able to log into your accounting software at any time. As your bookkeeper is keeping this up to date on a weekly basis, when you need paperwork urgently – for a loan, for example – your tax accountant can log into your accounting software and prepare the documents you need.

Your tax accountant should also discuss with you on a regular basis what your tax planning goals are. They should offer a tax planning meeting with you every year prior to the end of the financial year, around April or May, so you and your financial team know how you are tracking with your tax and can make adjustments to your plan if needed to make sure you get the best tax result possible.

They should also have an excellent relationship with your bookkeeper and Profit First Coach, so they can all work together to help you reach your goals with ease.

Your Profit First Coach

Your Profit First Coach should work with your team, and be in regular contact with your accountant and bookkeeper. Also note that your bookkeeper or accountant may be certified in Profit First, and this will mean they can help you with the bookkeeping or accounting and coach you around Profit First.

Your Profit First Coach can also be your virtual CFO. Just because you are a small business doesn't mean you don't need or can't have a CFO. For those tradies who have a business that they want to grow or are already at the stage where they have a team working with them, a virtual CFO can offer the extra financial guidance you need to succeed.

Your Profit First Coach will help you interpret your financials and work with you to create a financial map based on your needs and goals. They help teach you about the financial side of your business and set up strategies for you and your business to follow to help you achieve financial success.

YOU'RE THE BOSS

As you are the leader of this team, you are the one your chosen professionals are supporting to help you build the business you want. As the leader, it doesn't mean that you call all the shots, it means that you make sure your bookkeeper, accountant and Profit First Coach know what you want out of your business.

Is it more time with the family?

More profit in your pocket?

Being able to take a regular wage?

Being able to take a holiday and not have to work yourself into the ground to catch up?

This list can be endless, and it is your job to figure out what you want so your financial team can help you get it, which is why we discussed your goals in chapter 6. Once you know what your ultimate goal is, your financial team can help you break that down, and each of them can take control of their part and help educate you to be able to make better decisions in your business.

Education is the key to unlocking success in your business. Education helps you become more efficient. When you know better you can do better. It also allows you to make decisions more quickly than you could before because you have the required knowledge, which means you have more certainty. When you have certainty you have action, and when you have action you have progress. When you have progress your goals become much more achievable than they ever were.

Once you hit one milestone, you start gaining momentum and the next one comes more quickly. This keeps compounding until you have such momentum that business becomes much easier and much more enjoyable. The quickest way to turn a business around or to get a business off the ground is to find people who have had success with other clients in the areas you need and to work with them.

Invest in yourself and your business wisely with the right team and the benefits that follow will help you move from a struggling business owner to a successful one who has a business that works for them and not a business that works you to the bone. A high number of small business owners, particularly tradies, work very long hours, and if they took a minute to look at their actual hourly rate they would realise that financially they would be better getting a job. But for many people, getting a job is out of the question for a number of reasons, and that is perfectly okay. But that doesn't mean you need to keep struggling doing ridiculous hours working for yourself if you are making less money that you would be at a job.

GET STARTED...

Do you love working with your tax accountant? **Y/N**

Do you love your current bookkeeping arrangements? **Y/N**

Now, if you hesitated in answering these questions or answered *no* then start a list of what isn't currently working so you know what you will need to look for when you make the move.

Part III

PREPARE

Chapter 9

GETTING THE NUMBERS RIGHT

GETTING THE FOUNDATIONS RIGHT

I am yet to meet a tradie who jumps for joy when we discuss their bookkeeping. I am usually met with a deep sigh and something along the lines of, 'I know I should have this under control', or, 'I've tried to keep it up to date but I have been so busy with jobs that I just haven't had time'. Most people – let alone tradies – don't like bookkeeping. In fact, many hate it because in their experience it has been hard, complicated and uninteresting. Even though you know it's vital to have your bookkeeping up to date, you just can't find a way to do it.

Getting the numbers right in your business is just as important as getting the foundation right of a new house build. If the foundation isn't right and hasn't followed the plan, problems will start to occur. Sometimes if you are lucky these problems appear years down the track and are only small cracks that appear in the gyprock, and the owner luckily passes it off as the house settling. You escape having to come back and fix the job, and it doesn't cost you anything, or at worst maybe a phone call from the owner asking if this is normal.

But if these little cracks start to grow to a point where the owner can no longer tolerate them, the once pleasant home owner can turn into a very frustrated and angry client. You will have to go back and remedy the problems, and this can cost you anywhere from a thousand dollars if you take into consideration your time and effort to thousands and maybe even tens of thousands of dollars, depending on what the issue is.

In getting your bookkeeping right, you have the best intentions and you do what you know to be right at each stage. You may even have had advice from your accountant or other business owners who have more established businesses than you. You followed their lead and took their advice and thought you were on the right track – until you received a letter or phone call from the ATO chasing you for an outstanding BAS, or it could be from personal tax you forgot all about paying even though you have a vague recollection of it.

When you get your numbers right and have exceptional bookkeeping practices it is far less stressful for you, which allows you to concentrate on getting your jobs done to the high standard you expect. And focusing on doing great work means you get more work. Word of mouth recommendations are still one of the very best ways to get new and consistent work.

YOUR FINANCIAL DOCUMENTATION

I am yet to find a tradie who is excited at the thought of reading their profit and loss statement and balance sheet, which are given to them usually after paying the bill to their tax accountant at the end of the financial year. The role of a tax accountant has traditionally been to complete your end-of-financial-year tax work, which results in them providing you with the profit and loss, balance sheet and potentially some other documents – often you have no idea what they all mean. And that is normal.

To implement Profit First successfully we need these documents, and we love great tax accountants who are able to do this work for you to provide these. We don't go into teaching you the ins and outs of what these documents mean; we do however use the information in these reports to prepare our profit assessment for your business. We use this information to create your individualised profit assessment, which then helps us work out your CAPs and your TAPs, and finally helps us to work with you on an ongoing basis to set up Profit First successfully in your business.

BOOKKEEPING BASICS

With the technology available to us today your bookkeeping can be much more efficient than it has ever been. Gone are the days when you need to collect your paper receipts and take them to your bookkeeper or accountant, where someone would have to sit down and waste hours of time to enter all the information into your bookkeeping system.

But there are so many choices available that I find sometimes people become overwhelmed and then don't do anything, putting them right back into the spot they so desperately wanted to get out of. You are left feeling like it's all too hard, and you go back to doing what you are good at and leave this for 'another day'.

The problem is, days turn into weeks, which turn into months and years, and before you know it your bookkeeping is a huge mess and you don't know where to turn to get help or if you can ever get out of this.

Let's have a look at how you can avoid this scenario.

Step 1: Make a decision

The first decision is not about what you need to do but who you need to help you with getting this all sorted out.

Imagine you are a cabinet maker and you have quoted a job to make and install an amazing kitchen for a new client, yet after sending the quote you don't hear back from them. When they finally do respond, they tell you they had a handyman install a Bunnings kitchen for them instead. Now, at no point in time did they tell you this was a consideration; in fact, if they had, maybe you wouldn't have spent so long on the quote. You know that the quality of both the kitchen and the installation won't be anywhere near the quality that you could have provided, yet the client can't see your value in the job. The Bunnings kitchen the client chose instead of the custom kitchen you were going to install for them will do the job okay for now, but in the long run it will start to show signs of wear and tear much earlier that your custom kitchen.

If you are doing your own bookkeeping then you are the handyman in that story. You know you can't do as good a job as an outstanding bookkeeper, yet you do it anyway because you are trying to save money or you just haven't had the time to find a bookkeeper.

Make the decision to hire a bookkeeper, and then find one. An outstanding bookkeeper will save you enormous amounts of not only time but also money in the long run, as they will assess your business and set up not only apps and programs that will save you time on your bookkeeping, but an outstanding bookkeeper will also offer suggestions on other areas of your business which you need to look at. They have the knowledge and experience to look at your business and help guide you in what else and who else you may need to help.

Step 2: Review your current bookkeeping

One of the main contributors to the high number of failures tradies have in business is the fact that there isn't an efficient and effective bookkeeping system in place. Used to its full potential, a great system will make sure your bookkeeping is efficient and therefore effective, which will greatly reduce the chance of your business failing. It will also provide a number of valuable reports and data to improve decision making in your business.

Ask any accountant, bookkeeper or business owner which bookkeeping program is right for your business and you'll get a range of different answers, from Xero, MYOB and QuickBooks to Excel spreadsheets. You'll also get a range of reasons why, from cost to ease of use to 'that's what so-and-so recommended'. The list is long, daunting and at times confusing, and this can be frustrating when you take into account that making the right choice could dramatically improve your business and your lifestyle.

In my bookkeeping business, Efficient Tradie, we use and recommend Xero as I believe it is the best on the market for tradies.

The first thing we do at Efficient Tradie when we have a new client is review their current systems and processes and recommend solutions based on our review of their current systems and processes and of what the business needs.

When reviewing and researching a bookkeeping system, you need to ask yourself a number of questions, including:

☐ What does my business do? (Do I have a storefront trades business? Do I sell online? Do I need to control stock? Do I have in-house staff or field staff? Do I need to track my staff time on jobs? And so on.)

☐ Do I only need to access my system from the office? Will I want to access it when I am outside the office?

☐ What information do I need to record?

☐ Do I want to be able to 'see' where my business is financially at any point in time?

☐ How can I make receipt management easy?

☐ Do I love chasing up outstanding invoices for money that my business is owed?

☐ Would I like to grow my business?

☐   Does my business need to make me more money?

☐   Do I know how much money I am making in my business at the moment?

☐   What are the comparative costs of the systems?

Do you really need a new system?

Tradies don't go into business to get bogged down in paperwork and bookkeeping tasks – but they're nuisances we all need to deal with when working for ourselves. For most business owners, more free time is something we'd come close to trading our firstborn for.

Thanks to the rise in cloud accounting, we can get our essential bookkeeping tasks done in less time than ever. Here are ten reasons why people are getting onto the cloud-wagon and choosing Xero:

1. **It's super accessible:** You can access all of your essential financial information from anywhere and at any time, provided you have an internet connection. Best of all, this means your accountant and bookkeeper can access the same current information at any time – without carting bulky paperwork around!

2. **It's inexpensive:** Xero requires you to pay a low monthly fee, as opposed to forking out a fortune upfront for a traditional program.

3. **It's automated:** No more hours spent inputting each and every receipt and invoice before reconciling! Xero takes advantage of automatic bank feeds, which are updated each night directly from your bank account to Xero. Reconciling is made easy, with automatic matching of bank transactions.

4. **It automatically updates and upgrades:** This means you don't have to do anything – the software does it all in the cloud, giving you more time.

5. **It automatically backs up your information:** Xero is popular because the backup process is completely automated. There is one single source of information, consistently backed up to avoid the risk of data loss. No more traditional, manual backups.

6. **All the information at your fingertips is current and accurate:** The fact that Xero interfaces with your bank statements means that the information stored in the cloud software is totally current. In just minutes, you can create any information files you're likely to need if you're applying for finance. It's great for information gathering at tax time as well.

7. **It provides a clean audit trail:** All of your financial records are at your fingertips, and your data won't be compromised. Every business transaction is recorded, including sales contracts, payments to employees, tax and superannuation. This is what potential investors want to see!

8. **You can get started quickly, easily and confidently:** Most cloud-based accounting software provides you with a really simple dashboard, so you don't need to do a course just to navigate and operate the program. Easy online tutorials are there to help you every step of the way too.

9. **It gives you out-of-box reports without the box:** Interfacing with your bank account means no more sorting through boxes and files to find that statement that arrived months ago. One click and it's right there.

10. **It syncs with other business applications:** When you use cloud-based software, you'll be able to take advantage of apps that sync with your financial data. Using apps to handle inventory management, invoicing and a whole lot more can take the time and hassle out of accounting.

Switching to cloud accounting will not only save you time, it will also support the strong financial foundation you can build through the steps to come.

Step 3: Set up your new bookkeeping process

One of the big questions you need to ask yourself at this stage is:

Do I want to outsource my bookkeeping?

I am a big believer in the only way businesses can be successful is to have the best people doing their best work so we can do our best work. In my business, originally it was just me. However, I soon realised that if I wanted to grow my business and help the number of tradies I wanted to, I had to 'let go' and outsource most of the day-to-day activities in my business. I had to stick to doing what I was good at for two reasons:

☐ When you are able to focus on what you are good at and just do that, you become outstanding at that. And you get to do the fun stuff in your business day in and day out.

☐ Financially, even though I was paying others to do work I could have done, they are going to be much better and more efficient at those tasks than I ever would be.

Nobody wants to be a jack of all trades and a master of none.

Outsourcing doesn't mean I dump the activities on someone else and let them loose; quite the opposite. You have to do the work to start with and set clear expectations and guidelines on exactly what you expect of each person.

For example, when we take on a new bookkeeping client we provide them with a checklist of what we will be doing for them each week, month, quarter and year so that they know exactly what they are getting and when. It makes it crystal clear for both parties who is doing what and by when. As we have a process in place, both my team at Efficient Tradie and the tradie are able to get on with the job and aren't wasting time following up who is doing what and what hasn't been done yet.

Now, whether you hire someone who works from your office or someone who works from their office, you need to make sure that this person 'fits' your business and that you can work with them. At Efficient Tradie we set clear expectations and regularly review outcomes to make sure not only our client is getting what they need but also so my business continues to thrive.

As we all know, time is precious, and you never seem to have enough hours in the day. You may already work over ten hours a day and still not get everything you need done – how are you going to find the time to do the research required to find an outstanding bookkeeper?

Here are two options you can take to find an outstanding bookkeeper:

☐ Ask your colleagues, friends and family for recommendations. Make sure you ask them if they have or do they know of an *outstanding* bookkeeper. You don't want a good bookkeeper or even a great bookkeeper, you want someone who is at the top of their field, someone who can become part of your financial team (as we covered in chapter 8).

☐ Feel free to email me (Katie@profitfirstfortradies.com.au with the subject: Bookkeeping Help) and I will happily book a time for you to have a chat to see what Efficient Tradie can offer you and your business. We are a certified Profit First bookkeeping business and can help make the transition to Profit First even simpler. Check out www.profitfirstfortradies.com.au/bookkeeping if you would like to find out more about how we support our tradies in their bookkeeping.

It's important to find a bookkeeper who fits with what your business needs, and if you are reading this book you are more than likely thinking about implementing Profit First in your business. Be sure that anyone you consider for your bookkeeping is certified in Profit First, otherwise you will have complications as they will be unfamiliar with your Profit First goals and strategy, making the Profit First journey more difficult than it needs to be.

I don't entirely agree with the saying 'you need to spend money to make money'. I believe you need to invest money to make money. Investing in an outstanding bookkeeper is a valuable step for your business, and the results will pay you back tenfold when you invest in the right person.

Often tradies baulk at paying for a bookkeeper. When I dig a little deeper it is usually because they've had a bad experience with an average bookkeeper who has cost them time and – even worse – money in the past. I went through this in my business as well. The list of reasons I had for why I couldn't outsource my marketing (which is my least favourite thing to do in my business) was long, very long. Overall, I decided I'd be unable to afford it. I also felt guilty at the thought of outsourcing any part of my business. Many thousands of business owners before me had struggled through having to 'do it all'. They survived; why couldn't I? Did I think I was worse than them if I chose to outsource? If I chose to relieve some of the pressure? What would I talk about when a bunch of business owners were standing around discussing the hours upon hours they spend a day devoted to their business?

But I realised that just because something has always been done a certain way, it doesn't mean we have to keep doing it that way.

If we want change, we have to step outside our comfort zones.

The biggest problem I had was getting over myself – getting out of my own way and allowing myself to at least try another way. What did I have to lose?

Outsourcing can be a scary topic, especially when we talk about outsourcing any part of our financials, yet in almost all successful small businesses they are outsourcing their bookkeeping. Now, I am not saying hand it all over to the bookkeeper and never look at you numbers – absolutely not. I am strongly suggesting that you hand it over to your bookkeeper and educate yourself about your numbers. You don't have to learn everything all at once, but once you have a system set up you will find it is much easier to learn about the numbers when it is simple and organised.

Yes, it could all fall in a heap. The person you outsource to could make an absolute mess of your bookkeeping, but if you choose wisely that's not going to happen. And if what you are doing now isn't working for you, you need to take the time to make a change. Working with a Profit First bookkeeper will be your best bet.

THE BENEFITS OF AUTOMATION

When you have chosen the right bookkeeping system and had it set up by a professional, they will have also set up Xero – for example – to make use of the various automation tools available, which not only makes your bookkeeping more efficient but also more effective.

When Sam came to Efficient Tradie as a client he had been using Xero for a little while. He mentioned to me that he didn't think he would have to answer his bookkeeper's questions every week about how certain transactions should be processed, and could I have a look to see if there was a better option. It took Sam all of 30 seconds to give me access to his Xero account, and while we were on the phone I was reviewing his bookkeeping for him.

Unfortunately he had been using a bookkeeper who wasn't up to date with the automation side of Xero, such as bank feeds. Bank feeds are where you authorise your bank to electronically send your bank transactions directly into your accounting software each night, Monday to Friday, so they are ready and waiting for your bookkeeper.

I noticed he was also using Receipt Bank, which is a receipts management tool, but noticed the automation hadn't been set up, which is why Sam would have been getting all the questions from the previous bookkeeper. Receipt Bank wasn't being used to its full potential, nor was Xero.

Both Receipt Bank and HubDoc allow you to take a photo of your receipts and upload them into the program where you or your bookkeeper can specify what account they should go to. You can also select for these to be automated, so for example any time a receipt is received from BP it processes it to fuel costs. This not only saves a lot of time, it also removes the human error which can occur if a person is processing these receipts.

The reason I prefer and have used HubDoc for a number of years is HubDoc also fetches your bank statement at the end of the month. This allows us to double check the bank feed balance against the bank statement to make sure it is correct. While most banks have few problems with the feeds and the information is almost always correct, there are some banks that have issues with their feeds from time to time and this double check picks up on any errors quickly and they can be fixed.

I use HubDoc in my business because I find it the most efficient for the tradies I work with. There are other options like Receipt Bank. If you are working with a great bookkeeper they will have the knowledge to be able to review the options and find which would work best with you and your business.

Bank rules are another automation feature in Xero that can be helpful for transactions such as bank fees, as they are the same every month and you don't receive a receipt for them. By setting up a bank rule, you simply hit ok rather than having to type in who the transaction is from, what account it goes to and why it has occurred.

Xero has a number of other amazing features to help you make your bookkeeping efficient and effective. If you would like to know more please visit www.profitfirstfortradies.com.au/xero.

QUICK AND EFFICIENT QUOTING

Quoting a job is an important and often overlooked piece of the financial puzzle, and is often done quickly for a number of reasons. Tradies are busy and don't have the time to waste on a quote, so they throw something together, add a bit on in case they get it and hope for the best. This is often the start of the cash flow issues they encounter down the track. This is common practice; you are not alone if this is how you are quoting.

I hear time and time again from the tradies we work with that they thought they had 'put enough on top to cover the job' or they 'missed the email about the steel price increase' and didn't realise they hadn't allowed enough. By this stage they are often deflated and at their wits end. But when I ask them about their quoting process there is rarely actually a process that they follow. This is through no fault of their own; it is often because they didn't know there was a better way.

At Efficient Tradie we use and recommend Xero as I believe it is the best on the market for my tradies. It talks to a large number of other apps and programs that our tradies can use to make their life easier and more efficient. If you don't use Xero I strongly recommend you check it out. If you use other software you should have similar capabilities as I discuss here for Xero.

There are two ways to do your quoting efficiently, and it will depend on the size of your business and your ability to look at options other than using the quote function in Xero.

The first option, using the quote function in Xero, has a number of benefits:

☐ You don't need to have or learn other software.

☐ It is quick and easy for you to send a quote as there are email templates you can use to save time.

☐ Your client receives both a PDF copy of the quote and a link. They can accept your quote simply by clicking the link, and your quote automatically turns into an invoice.

- ☐ If they have a question they can press the comment button and their question will be sent to you, making it easier for them as they don't have to go back to their emails and write an email.

- ☐ To turn an accepted quote into an invoice, you only need to press one button and the invoice is created without any further work from you.

The downsides to using the Xero quote function are:

- ☐ If you are a larger trades business the quotes might be a little limiting for you if you often provide complex quotes.

- ☐ You don't have the function to enter detailed job costings that you can track against.

- ☐ If you want to track job costs you quote on based on price lists from your suppliers or association, it becomes a little too complex and time consuming for Xero to handle.

The second option is that you use an add-on. An add-on is an app or program that has been designed for a specific industry such as builders, plumbers or concreters. There is also a range of different add-ons that service different-sized tradies. For example, Tradify and ServiceM8 suit a number of different trades but are better for the smaller tradie, whereas add-ons such as Simpro meet the needs of more complex larger trades businesses.

The world of add-ons is vast, and at the time of writing this book, the number of app partners listed in the Xero directory for construction and trades had over 50 different options, each specialising in their various areas. As ever, different businesses have different needs, and it is often difficult to navigate through this list and to know where to start. When I'm working with my clients, we often uncover areas where they have a glitch that is taking up their precious time and causing them enormous amounts of stress as they often need to engage in using one of the apps, but they are stopped because of the overwhelm that comes with trying to figure out which one is going to fix their problem.

Early on in my business journey I met Clinton Cowin, the founder of TradiePad, a technology training company that shows tradies how to use mobile devices and cloud-based software to revolutionise the way they do business. They help their clients sort through the vast number of apps and help them find a customised solution for their business. They save the business owner time and money by helping them either eliminate the paper-based way they are working or helping them set up a technology-based system to have everything they need online and at their fingertips.

If you feel like you could benefit from a chat with Clinton or his team at TradiePad then I strongly suggest you add it to your To Achieve list as it will help change your business. It will also mean that you have even more data for your Profit First journey, which makes mapping out and making decisions even easier.

What you use to present your quote is important. Even more important is what information you use and how you calculate your quote. Now, I am not going to pretend to be the master quote creator; you the tradie would have far more experience than I would at preparing quotes. There are, however, some basics that I find tradies mention to me time and time again that they forget about, so I will highlight them here in case you are making the same mistakes.

As you will see, most of these – if not all – are pretty basic, but tradies are so busy with the 101 things they are trying to juggle that some things slip through the cracks. If this can be a reminder to you so that you don't get caught short on a quote again then my job is done:

☐ **Use the most up-to-date price list from your supplier.**
I know that seems obvious, but the number of times I have heard, 'Damn, I must have used the old price list' – well, I have lost count. Contact all your suppliers and ask them to add you to their list that they email when they have a new price list available. Destroy the old price list as soon as you get a new one. Again, I know this seems like an obvious thing to do, but the number of stories I have heard about tradies losing money because they used the wrong price list is huge.

- ☐ **Make sure you have all the information you need from your client to quote the job.** Don't be afraid to ask a lot of questions when you are visiting the client and the site gathering information for the job. The more information you have, the more accurate the quote will be. I know quotes are often done at the end of the day and you just want to get home, but by spending a little more time at this stage you will save yourself enormous amounts of time and money down the track. It will also set you apart from other tradies who are quoting the job, as many don't do this step and your potential client will notice you asked more questions than the others and they will assume you have a better idea of what you are doing. Potentially you could increase your sales at this stage too as a result.

- ☐ **Set aside uninterrupted time to do your quotes.** I can hear you saying 'yeah, right', and I understand that. But one of the most common comments my tradies make is that they rushed to get a quote done and stuffed it up, big time.

- ☐ **Set your quotes to be valid for 30 days only and subject to supplier price changes.** This gives you the opportunity to not have to honour a quote after the 30-day mark, or if there is a price jump within that 30 days you can amend your quote to the client to make sure you cover the increased cost to you.

- ☐ **Send your quotes promptly.** Again, this will set you apart from the other tradies vying for the job, as most take too much time and the client assumes that if they are slow to get the quote back they will be slow to do the job. An additional step to this would be to do a follow-up email, phone call or text the following day asking them to confirm they received the quote and letting them know you are contactable if they have any questions, and if you don't hear from them within a certain number of days that you will send them a quick follow-up email or text to see if there is anything else they need.

Making sure you have done these five things will set you apart from 99% of the other tradies, it will increase your chances of getting the job, and you will also be showing the client that you are organised and on top of your paperwork. This will help when it comes to invoicing and payment time as they will already know you are efficient with your paperwork and will be prompted to follow up your payment. (More on that in the invoice section below.)

These five simple steps will make a huge difference to your business. If you don't get your quotes right you start the ball rolling on what can become a boulder so big it will crush your business and its cash flow for years to come. Quoting well is the first step in setting your business up for success, and when done correctly changes not only your business but your whole attitude towards your business.

I'm sure you've had occasions when you quoted poorly and had to honour the quote. How does that job end up going? It's always stressful and usually fraught with even more problems that seem to be taking endless amounts of money out of your pocket 'just to keep the client happy'. Too many of these and you will find yourself stressed and broke.

QUICK AND EFFICIENT INVOICING

My phone rang, and when I answered I heard a very uncomfortable voice. Steve was after a new bookkeeper as his bookkeeping had gotten away from him and he needed a hand. He asked me all the standard questions, and even after I answered them all he still sounded quite stressed, which is not unusual. I then asked him how his cash flow was.

Silence.

Then more silence.

The length of silence that follows that question gives me a good indication of just how bad it is. I realised that this client had a huge cash flow issue. The silence was one of the longest I had endured, until he finally said, 'I've been working flat out but have no cash. I've got no idea why.'

I met with Steve and went through his bookkeeping, and while a little messy and behind, it wasn't the worst I have seen. The state of his bookkeeping wasn't matching the stress he had about his cash flow.

That's when I looked at his outstanding invoices figure.

It was over $70,000.

No wonder Steve had a cash flow issue.

When I dug into the outstanding invoice list I noticed that they were all from the same client, a large, well-known client who – going by the payment dates – paid approximately 60 to 90 days from the invoice date. These jobs weren't small jobs and required my client to pay for supplies and labour for each job and then move onto the next job. He was floating his large, well-known client to the tune of more than $70,000, and it was sending him broke and into a place mentally that was not pretty.

The first question I asked was, how long after a job has been completed do you send the invoice? He replied that he always sends the invoice the day after the job is signed off without fail, as he knows how long it takes to get these paid. That is perfect, and how it should be done for every job. Finish the job – send the invoice within 24 hours of job completion. If that is difficult for you to do, you need to review why and fix whatever is holding you up on this.

The second question I asked was, how often do you follow up said large client to see when they are going to make payment? 'Never,' was his response. We all know the saying 'the squeaky wheel gets the oil'. Steve wasn't making even the littlest of squeaks, which is one of the main reasons he was getting paid so late.

When you have a major client, I suggest that you become friendly with the accounts person. Always be kind and courteous, even if they are dragging out payment and you are ready to lose your mind. People have long memories, and if you lose it with the accounts person they will put you to the bottom of the pile and pay your invoice when they are ready. This may not be every accounts person, but from surveying my clients who have this issue it seems to be fairly common practice. When chasing up an invoice, I suggest a phone call over an email, as it is much harder for the accounts person to keep giving you excuses over the phone than to just send off a quick email saying it will be paid in a certain period of time.

I recommend that my clients set up the following for their invoices:

☐ Make sure you have given your client a copy of your terms and conditions (T&Cs), and that they have signed or acknowledged that they accept these terms. These can be on your quote, so when they accept the quote they are also accepting your T&Cs. I highly recommend you have your T&Cs written up by a professional who specialises in this area.

☐ Take a deposit where possible to book in the job.

☐ Set out stages of the job and expected payment amounts for each stage.

☐ Invoice each stage as it happens. If you finish the stage today, make sure your invoice for this stage is sent within 24 hours. Do not delay this step. Sending your invoices out on time is the first step in making sure you are paid on time. If you move onto the next phase of the job and the due date passes and it is not paid, nicely inform the client that you can't continue until you are paid the outstanding amount. Don't be afraid to do this.

☐ Email a reminder five days after the invoice was due. Again, always be polite.

☐ Make a phone call seven days after the invoice due date. Kindly ask them when you can expect payment. They more often than not will give you a date. Thank them for their time and mention that you will give them a quick call the day after the due date to let them know it has been received. This does two things: it lets them know that you are serious about getting this money sooner rather than later, and it also puts it in their head that if they aren't paid on the date they stated that you will be calling the day after again and they will have to come up with an excuse as to why it hasn't been paid.

☐ Ring the day after they said it was due if it is not in your account. Again, this shows them you mean business and you are becoming the squeaky wheel. In this phone call, again be nice and mention that the payment hasn't been received and you just want to check that it was paid in case the payment has gone missing. You may get a valid response as to the delay so again keep it cool and be polite. Again, ask when you can expect payment, thank them for the call, and let them know you will give them a quick call the day after they said they would pay to let them know that it has been received.

Repeat this process until you get paid. Now, it might seem like a pretty simple process, and it is; the problem is if you aren't doing it you are not top of the pile when your clients are paying bills. If you don't follow them up you are at the bottom of the pile and they will pay you when they get to you.

It is also handy to have someone else make the phone calls for you, as this keeps your relationship with the client strictly job related. We follow up invoices on behalf of many of our clients when needed and find that as we are the bookkeeper the client is much more relaxed and understanding as it is 'our job' to follow these things up.

With my client Steve, that is exactly what I did – I became so friendly with Steve's client's accounts person that she started calling me if the invoice wasn't getting paid when she had said it would be and she would give me another date without me having to ask.

Finally, after about four months of this process, I received a call from Steve's large client. To my surprise, she was calling to let me know that all the invoices that were outstanding had been paid and they would be in the account tomorrow. I asked her for the invoice numbers that had been paid so I knew what to expect payment for.

What she meant by 'all accounts' included the two invoices which had only been sent in the last two weeks. It was 22 December, and my client was about to receive a very large sum of money into his account before Christmas for the work he and his team had done. I thanked her very much, wished her a Merry Christmas and New Year and hung up the phone. At this stage I wasn't 100% sure that it would occur. I mentioned to Steve about the phone call and his response was, 'Yeah right, I'll wait to see that'.

The text I received from Steve at 6:30 am the following morning isn't fit for publication, safe to say he was very pleased that he had been paid in full, including the most recent invoices. This cycle continued into the new year. Steve was now being paid within 30 days of submitting his invoices, and he was over the moon. His cash flow was restored, and he was able to start doing things in the business he had always dreamed of but couldn't because he was so restricted by this client and the cash flow crisis they were causing.

I am more than aware that in the construction industry that you as a tradie work in not all stories have a good result like Steve's. There are and will always be sharks in the industry who have very little intention of paying you on time, and some who have no intention of paying you at all. This is why it is important to follow up your invoices, as you can quickly decide to stop doing any more work if there's an issue. You then have the option to send the invoice to a debt collector or cut your losses.

You should also make sure you have water-tight terms and conditions in place to increase your chances of being able to get all or at least some of your money back if a client holds back payment. If you are owed money, you have the legal right to request payment for the work completed. It is common for clients to take advantage of your good nature and tell you that they are not happy with the price after you have completed the job. This is another reason why it is vital to provide a detailed quote to the client and make sure you have it in writing – either electronically or on paper – that they not only accept the job and what it entails but also that they accept your terms and conditions.

It makes following up outstanding invoices much easier when you have provided a detailed quote that included your terms and conditions. It also makes it a much easier process if you need to get a debt collector to collect the debt for you, as you have followed the correct procedure. If you have to take it to mediation or court, in having a detailed quote along with your terms and conditions signed and accepted by the client, you are much better placed for a positive outcome.

Your terms and conditions are an important document that needs to be prepared by a lawyer or an appropriate body so that you know they are correct and will stand up in court if need be. It also shows the client once again that you are organised and on the ball. If you are a member of an association they should be able to help you out with this.

You should also make it easy for your clients to pay you. Make sure you have a number of payment options available to them.

'BLOODY BILLS'

'Bloody bills'. I hear my tradies say this often. Getting bills in your business is inevitable; as long as you're doing the jobs you are going to have bills of some description. At Efficient Tradie we love making this step seamless and easy for you as we know how much you hate dealing with the receipts. Gone are the days of stuffing your receipts in a shoe box and handing them to the bookkeeper at the end of the month or quarter for them to sit down and spend hours and hours data entering them into your bookkeeping system.

As I mentioned earlier, at Efficient Trade we recommend Hub-Doc, which is an app our tradies use to take a photo of their receipts and it then sends all the information through to Xero for us to double check. The time saved by investing in HubDoc each month is enormous, even for the smallest of tradies, let alone those who have larger businesses. For those bills you receive by email, all you do is forward them on to your HubDoc email address and it goes through the same process. No need to even print them and take a photo of them.

The reason I love HubDoc and this process so much is this is where I find most tradies are caught out and end up paying more GST and other taxes than they need to. For every receipt that is lost and you have no proof as per the ATO requirements, technically you shouldn't be claiming it. For those who do, you run the risk of an ATO audit and the potential for them to not allow these claims, which results in a tax adjustment that you weren't expecting, and maybe penalties as well.

That is never a fun situation, which is why we use HubDoc and make sure all our tradies get into the habit of snapping a photo of every physical receipt or sending the email direct to HubDoc, as by doing so not only is the information from the bill scanned and uploaded into Xero for you automatically, a photo of the bill is also kept in HubDoc and Xero for you for compliance purposes, which keeps the ATO very happy.

GET STARTED...

Review your current bookkeeping program by writing a dot-point list of what it doesn't do for you and your business at the moment.

Chapter 10

GETTING THE BUSINESS MANAGEMENT RIGHT

MANAGING YOUR PURCHASING

An area of business that is often overlooked as a place to become more efficient and organised is in your purchasing. Unfortunately as humans we can be disorganised, which not only costs us time but also money. That quick trip to Bunnings to grab a few lengths of timber you were short soon becomes an hour trip and you walk out with an armful of other bits and pieces you don't necessarily need but grabbed 'just in case'. The problem is they get thrown in the ute or truck and are often not used for weeks or months, or often not used at all.

The more time you spend on the quoting step, the more time and money you save in this step. If you do a detailed quote, it not only allows you to make sure you have covered off everything required for the job but it allows you to order the materials for the job much more easily and with far less waste. In fact, if you are using an add-on program for your quoting, for many of them you can with the click of a button have your purchases list for all the materials for the job.

If you have a clear idea from the start what you need for the job and then follow the list buying the materials when needed rather than as you go, you will find you are saving time and are able to spend more time on the site. More time on the site means more time to get the job done more quickly, which results in the job getting finished quicker. If the job is finished quicker you get paid sooner. It's not complicated but is often overlooked because you are so busy chasing your tail.

You won't change everything overnight and make it perfect, but you can make it easier if you start taking small steps each day to make new habits once you are aware of how easy it can be to make such a difference to your business.

The other area of purchasing which is important is making sure you are getting the best deal from your suppliers. For many tradies the trades supply businesses are limited, and it feels like you don't have a choice but to pay the price they offer you. That is not the case. You just have to take some time and seek out a better deal. Now I know you are thinking, 'who has time for that?', but it can be as simple as a phone call or a quick chat when you are in there next.

For example, I have had a number of tradies who work with me who use Bunnings for most of their supplies as Bunnings has so many stores, which makes it convenient. Many haven't had accounts with Bunnings as they haven't jumped through all the hoops and paperwork needed. What they didn't know is that they could apply for a Bunnings PowerPass card, which isn't an account so it doesn't need all the paperwork but it does give them a percentage off their purchases. It is these little savings which add up to large savings over time. That money is better in your business than in Bunnings.

For those tradies who have accounts with various suppliers they often overlook the timing of the purchases. I hear story after story of tradies ordering materials and having them delivered to a job site days or weeks before the job starts. This means those materials are on your account, and the clock is ticking for when you have to pay for them. If you aren't starting the job for days or weeks, you are losing that time and will find yourself paying for materials well before the invoice is paid. Hello cash flow issues.

Time management is often a problem on job sites because you are usually one of a number of trades on the job and you are often held up because of someone else. There are going to be times when this happens and things are out of your control. Now, imagine you ordered materials early and then you are delayed by another trade; you now have materials sitting on site unable to be used and you are having to pay for them.

GET STARTED...

Try this experiment: focus on how you manage the purchasing of your materials for just one month. I guarantee you will become more aware of your process. This allows you to review the process and make improvements. Yes, it may take a little extra time during the month, but the benefit of building new and improved habits will pay you back over and over well into the future.

STAFFING AND SUBBIE SUCCESS

Staffing and success aren't usually words I hear my tradies use in the same sentence. Staffing – and I include getting subbies to work for you – is difficult for almost all businesses I talk to, even those not in the trades industry. Good staff and subbies can be difficult to attract and even harder to retain, yet you need them if you want to run a business that isn't just you as an owner operator.

If you want to build a business that makes you not only turnover but a profit and doesn't run you into the ground, you are going to need help. After working with so many tradies over the years, I see certain consistent patterns that arise when dealing with staff and subbies. There will be days when they don't turn up and won't notify you, there are days when they leave early and don't tell you, and there are times when they stop showing up altogether without notice and stop answering your calls and messages.

This often happens in the middle of a big job when you need them most, just like it did for Paul who has a plumbing business with three staff and he uses subbies as he needs them depending on the size of the job. In the middle of a decent job with a new, well-connected client, one of Paul's staff members sent a text to Paul saying he didn't believe he was being paid the right hourly rate and also that his overtime was wrong. Paul replied that he would look into it for him and get back to him. Paul got busy and a few days had passed when he arrived one morning to the job site of this new and well-connected client to find none of his staff on site. But his client was.

You can imagine the conversation with the new client as to why the site had been empty for three hours that morning. Paul had no answer. His staff member who he didn't get back to had also spoken with the other two, and they had all decided not to show up that day and not tell Paul as he hadn't responded to the text about the wages.

It had completely slipped Paul's mind, and he didn't realise how important it was to the staff member who raised it with him. After apologising to the new client and attempting to paint a nicer picture of what had occurred in an attempt to keep the client onside, Paul tried to call his staff but – no surprise – none of them answered their phones. He left each of them a message asking them to call him immediately. Now I understand that what the staff did in this situation may not have been their best choice, but this was the situation Paul had to deal with. Fortunately for him he had another plumber mate, Will, who had staff, so he called him hoping he would have some words of wisdom.

Will was a client of mine who – while he hadn't had staff not turn up on a job site when they should have – did have some experience he was able to share with Paul. When Will first became one of Efficient Tradie's bookkeeping clients, I suggested that he speak to an HR consultant who understood tradies to make sure he was covering off all the aspects he needed to be and to make sure he was paying his staff correctly. As a result, he found he wasn't actually paying their overtime correctly. Thankfully, he was able to get it fixed without too much issue from his staff as he brought it to their attention first. He had a solution for them and he paid the outstanding amounts.

Will explained to Paul what he had gone through and was able to connect Paul with the same HR consultant we had suggested who had helped Will. Paul made the phone call and spent the day sorting our his staffing mess. He was able to call his guys back later that day with a solution, and although he had to leave another message telling them he had it worked out they did call him back, and they were onsite and it was work as usual the next day.

I have found that those tradies who attract and retain great staff and subbies are those who have a more formal hiring process. Those who request a résumé with references and check the references can save themselves a lot of stress, as you can tell a number of things from a person's work history as well as their references.

I have also found those who have an induction process that includes running the staff or subbie through what is expected of them sets the scene for the employee. You make it clear to them what is and what isn't expected of them; for example:

☐ work hours

☐ how they log their hours

☐   when they will get paid

☐   if they use a work vehicle, what the expectations are around that.

The staff or subbie should also sign to confirm they have read and accepted these conditions. This allows you to have a checklist to come back to if this person doesn't abide by what they have agreed to. Having proper employment contracts set up is also vital, and I strongly suggest you speak to your association and have them guide you on this.

When you set clear expectations of your team, I have found you have a much better chance of being more successful in this area than before. Is it foolproof? No, but it is a vast improvement over having nothing at all.

Staffing can be very complicated and is often inadvertently overlooked in the daily pressures of running a business. But if you make a mistake in this area it can be very costly, which is why it's important to make sure you set up your staff correctly and understand what their entitlements are and make sure you pay all of those on time, every time.

Superannuation is one of those entitlements that I see time and time again not being paid at all, or at best very late. I suggest to all my tradies that they pay their staff's super every pay period, and for most that is weekly. It is not your money anyway and you should not be using their super money to help your cash flow. Since you are going to implement Profit First for Tradies in your business, you won't have this problem in the future. Xero allows you with the click of a few buttons to automatically pay the super by direct debit from your bank account. Take advantage of that function and make sure your super is paid every time.

Subbies is an often confusing area that trips up many tradies. Just because someone has an ABN or they say they are a subbie, that does not equal them actually being a subbie. They may technically be an employee. The ATO has an employee versus subcontractor tool which will step you through a number of questions and let you know what the result is. As long as you answer the questions accurately, it will let you know if each of your people is classed as a subbie or an employee. Often the answer is not what you want to hear and in fact that subbie is classed as an employee. There is no way around this; you must follow the ATO rules. If you don't and you are audited, you will be deemed to have not paid the correct entitlements and will be made to rectify the situation.

This tool as well as other resources can be found at www.profitfirstfortradies.com.au/toolkit.

DIGITAL SOLUTIONS

For those tradies who have staff or subbies on various sites or complex, larger scale jobs I always recommend taking the time to look at what your business needs so that you can find a solution that will help solve a problem you may be having. When I take on new bookkeeping or Profit First Coaching clients, many don't even realise they have a problem, let alone one that can be fixed with an app or program. The problem usually presents itself as the tradie having no time, or being 'swamped'. When I dig deeper this is usually as a result of a roadblock caused by a step in the client's processes.

Unfortunately, almost every tradie I have spoken to has the same issues and has no idea that there is a solution out there for them. The tradies I work with are often so busy 'getting the job done' they don't have time to research and find a solution. Some are so overworked they have nothing left at the end of the day, and the last thing they think of doing is finding a solution for a problem they think is very normal in their trade.

If you look at the app marketplace on the Xero website you will see there are hundreds of different programs to help you out with various roadblocks in your business. From time tracking apps to log staff or subbie hours, to job management software, to apps like

HubDoc which I mentioned earlier, just to name a few. There are also many other solutions available for other software platforms.

At Efficient Tradie we have specialists in our team to help you find what areas you need help with first. We then find a number of solutions for you and help you implement them in your business. We are partners for a number of key programs in the app marketplace that we know are the basics that every tradie needs.

For larger or more complex businesses, we have worked with Clinton and his team at TradiePad on a number of occasions to help our tradies get the services they need. By working with a company like TradiePad you are able to identify and implement the technology in your business much more quickly, which means you get to save yourself more time than you would have if you tried to implement it yourself.

As I mentioned earlier, your core financial team will consist of a bookkeeper, accountant and Profit First Coach who will work with your regularly. You can also have others such as TradiePad who will come in and work with you to implement the program or programs you need and then you move on.

GET STARTED...

There are many dates you need to be aware of when running a business; for example, when superannuation must be paid, or when your BAS is due. The list of dates is long and ever changing, so I've created an up-to-date list which you can print out so you can keep track of what is due and when. Go to www.profitfirstfortradies.com.au/toolkit.

Part IV

PROSPER

Chapter 11

PROTECT
AND PLAN

The final piece of the financial puzzle is to protect your working capacity through estate planning and personal insurance, such as life, total and permanent disability (TPD), trauma and income protection (IP), and plan for the future through superannuation and retirement planning strategies.

Neither of these topics are ones that we as a society generally talk about very often, and usually only once it is too late.

PROTECTING YOU AND YOUR FAMILY

Firstly, let's discuss protecting you and your family. I will break this into two sections: legal protection, such as wills, and personal insurance protection, death, TPD, trauma and IP insurance.

Wills

According to a recent article in *Money* magazine by Paul Clitheroe, over 50% of Australians do not have a current will and many more do not have a power of attorney, enduring guardianship and medical wishes documented to ensure that should anything happen that their wishes are carried out. Now, none of us like to think about having to use any of these documents, but not thinking about this does not equal 'it is not going to happen'. In fact, the odds are against us; the likelihood of having to use one of these documents is higher than not having to use them. And – eventually – we all have a need for them.

So, why do we avoid making the appointment with the solicitor to have these drawn up and executed?

Money.

Time.

Uncomfortableness.

As I have mentioned earlier in the book, before having my children I was a financial planner and I started out specialising in personal insurance. I loved that job because I knew I was making a difference to families in the event of something going horribly wrong. While it seems horrible to have to think about these types of things, imagine something happening and you not having any of these legal documents in place.

Mary and John were clients of mine when I first started in my financial planning role. Mary was a stay at home mum to three young children and John was the sole income earner. Unfortunately, they had a close family member who had suddenly passed away and left a young family similar to theirs in a mess because of not having a will in place, nor was there any personal insurance. Mary had watched her friend not only have to grieve the loss of her husband but also deal with the ramifications of not having the right protection. This extra workload that was placed on her as a result was not something Mary was willing to go through.

The uncomfortableness of talking about death or major sickness is usually backed up by 'we don't have the money now' or 'we just haven't found the time'; I heard this over and over again with my clients when I was a financial planner.

Unfortunately, these events don't wait for you to be ready, and often come when you least expect it.

I strongly suggest that you find a solicitor who specialises in estate planning and make an appointment. Don't put it off; make a phone call today.

Insurance

We insure our cars and our home without batting an eyelid, yet we rarely think about insuring our most valuable assets: us.

The value of our income over our working life compared to the value of our car or our home is enormous, yet we happily pay a couple of thousand dollars a year for our home insurance with the home worth, say, $600,000, yet baulk at the premiums for personal insurance which has the potential to provide us with much more protection.

Why is that?

Again I come back to the uncomfortableness about talking about death, disability, suffering a major trauma or having an injury or illness which prevents you from working for a long period of time. But I am here to tell you that no matter how difficult these topics are to discuss, you and your family will be very grateful that you have done so in the unfortunate event of one of these happening to you.

Unfortunately the financial planning industry has had its fair share of rogue advisers giving poor or substandard advice, as well as some of the companies providing these products not having clients' best interests at heart.

I will be honest: this certainly played a part in me not returning to my financial planning career after I had my children. It is unfortunate, because there are many amazing financial planners who truly do have their clients' best interests at heart. The recent Royal Commission into the Banking, Superannuation and Financial Services Industry has seen many issues uncovered, and has also seen many institutions making vast changes to ensure that their clients' best interests are always at the forefront.

Like any industry, there is good and bad. Please don't use this as a reason not to review your personal insurance options. Ask family and friends for recommendations for licensed advisers they have used. I have a small group of excellent advisers that I refer my clients to. These are advisers I have known for years and whose work speaks for itself. The feedback from these advisers' clients is only ever amazing, and these are the only advisers I will refer to. (I do not receive nor expect a 'kick back' for these referrals. I only refer to people who believe that referrals should be based on finding the right fit for our client.)

PLANNING

For many tradies, the thought of planning for their retirement is just a distant dream and one many of you tell me you will get to when it gets closer. When I was a financial planner, many of my business clients would come to me five to ten years out from retirement, ready to think about retirement planning. I always heard the same reasons: 'We have been too busy with the business', 'I don't really understand super', or my favourite, 'I'll get the old age pension anyway'.

Now these are all valid responses that could have been turned around with more education and interest from the business owner. It was one of the reasons I started my bookkeeping business, Efficient Tradie, which then led me to Profit First and building Profit First for Tradies. I saw this gap in their education and decided to do something about it.

In today's world, we all have access to whatever information we need on any topic we can think of. If we choose, we can take the time to educate ourselves about these things. Now, even though I find these topics interesting and fun, I am fully aware that not everyone shares my passion and that is why I decided to put this into this book.

When you implement Profit First in your trades business it will turn your business around, it will give you the opportunity to have the money to not only pay your wage but to also pay your superannuation as well. Since you now will have the money to pay your super, you want to make sure it is working as it should for you in the years between now and retirement age. No one wants to live only on the old age pension, so take control of your super money and invest it wisely. This is your first step in your retirement planning.

Superannuation became compulsory in the early '90s yet people still find super 'too confusing'. Why is that? I believe it's lack of education, so I would like to give you some hints and tips to get your started in the right direction.

Where are you now?

The first thing you need to do is get your current statement from your super fund. If you have more than one fund, now is a great time to look at your options for consolidating these. Have a look if there's any personal insurance included. Often there is default life and TPD. Have a look at what fees you are being charged, keeping in mind money going into super is taxed when it reaches your fund, at 15% rather than your marginal tax rate. Just start with these basics, one little step at a time.

Find an adviser

The next step I would like you to take is to find a licensed financial planner who specialises in working with super and personal insurance. The beauty here is you can see one licensed financial adviser and tick off both boxes.

To receive advice for personal insurance and super you need to make sure you speak with a *licensed* financial planner. A licensed financial planner will take the time to review your current situation and to really find out about your and your family's needs. They will then review what options are suitable for your unique situation and provide you with the appropriate advice. They will also step you through the application process to make sure that you do that correctly, which is an important step for both personal insurance and super.

For personal insurance, if the application process is short and doesn't ask for a full medical history of the applicant then you may have issues at the time of claim.

For super, if you don't have it set up correctly you may have a number of issues down the track, which is why I strongly suggest finding a licensed financial planner to help you through this process.

This is not a quick process and is not something that can be done over the phone in 15 minutes. Please avoid anything that is not advice based on your current situation, where the planner has completed an interview with you to gather all your details. 'All your details' is not only your name, phone number, address, age and smoking status. It includes things like your goals and dreams, your attitude towards risk, where are you now and where you want to be, and they will give your options on how you can get there.

I understand your days are busy with the 1,001 other things you need to do for your business, and I know by reading this book you will have added to that long list. So, what is another few things to add to that list, considering once these are done you will have the security of knowing you and your family will be taken care of if things go wrong? Or, better still, if they don't go wrong and you reach retirement in good health, you want to make sure your reward for working all those years is worth it.

You deserve that.

GET STARTED...

Step 1: Make an appointment to have your estate planning documents such as your will written or reviewed.

Step 2: Gather all your personal insurance statements and find out how much you have in the way of – or if you have – life, TPD, trauma and income protection insurance.

Step 3: Gather all your super statements and check the balances and if there is any insurance attached.

Step 4: Start looking for a licensed financial planner who can help you do a full review of your financial planning situation.

Chapter 12

GETTING STARTED WITH PROFIT FIRST CHECKLIST

☐ **Step 1:** Cut expenses. As explained in chapter 4, as you are now allocating money into your various accounts you will need to find some other funds from somewhere to cover your expenses. As a general rule we can usually cut 10% from a tradie's expenses without causing too much trouble.

☐ **Step 2:** Decide on your allocation day. In *Profit First* Mike refers to the 10th and the 25th. I find in Australia it is easier to do your allocations the day you do wages if you have staff or at least once per week, with the exception of those tradies such as builders who may get paid less frequently, then I suggest doing it once per fortnight.

☐ **Step 3:** Once you have chosen your day each week or fortnight, make sure you sit down at this time without fail and firstly add up the amount you have been paid in the time since your last allocation day and work out your percentage allocations. Once you have these percentages worked out, you can do your transfers for that period. You can download your allocation percentages calculator from www.profitfirstfortradies.com.au/toolbox.

☐ **Step 4:** The next step is to pay your bills from your Opex account only. More often than not you won't have enough money in your Opex to pay all your bills when you start your Profit First journey, and while this can be stressful, Profit First is just uncovering what was always there. Remember to take it step by step.

☐ **Step 5:** Quarterly profit distribution. Many would say this is the best part of Profit First. On the first of each month after the quarter finishes you are to sit down and look at the balance in the Profit account. This is your chance to reward yourself. 50% of what is in the Profit account is to be transferred to your personal account. It is to be spent on *you*, it is *not* to be spent on anything relating to the business. This is *your* reward for taking the risk and being the business owner. Enjoy it. The balance is to remain in the Profit account to save towards your rainy day/buffer account. Now, if you are paying off debt you can choose to use the funds from the Profit account to make a lump sum payment to your debt, but you must still transfer at least 1% to yourself as your reward.

Don't forget to celebrate once you have done each and every profit distribution.

☐ **Step 6:** Pay your BAS. Once you have set up Profit First and you have been putting aside 10% on each invoice being paid, you should have enough money to pay your BAS in full and on time. Another reason to celebrate. If you have extra funds in your BAS account you can choose to pay these towards your debts if you have them or keep them to add to your rainy day/ buffer fund. The goal of this fund is to build enough money to cover all of your expenses for at least three months. Once you reach the three-month mark, some tradies then aim to have six months or more covered. It is up to you. One thing you can be sure of is that once you have this buffer, business will feel a whole lot safer knowing you have this as back up should things slow down or something goes wrong and you need to take a break from the business.

☐ **Step 7:** Time to review your CAPs and move one step closer to your TAPs. Don't increase your CAPs too quickly. Mike suggests that you only move 3% each quarter. That could be from one account or 1% from three accounts. Remember, slow and steady wins the race.

☐ **Step 8:** Each April/May you should be having a tax planning meeting with your tax accountant. If you aren't, make sure you do this year. During this meeting they will be able to estimate what your tax position looks like and you can make sure that the tax percentage you are putting away each week will cover your end-of-year tax bill. This meeting gives you time to adjust or plan for your tax bill rather than getting a shock once your tax is completed.

GET STARTED...

Step 1: Keep a list of all the wins you have with Profit First, even the little wins, and make sure you review these often. Change can be harder for some than others, and this wins list will certainly help you if things are a little tough at stages.

Step 2: Make sure you have put time in your diary each week to do your allocations and pay your bills. You will be surprised at how quickly you are able to do your allocations and pay your bills once you get into the habit of it.

WHERE TO FROM HERE?

'The way to get started is to quit talking and begin doing.'

Walt Disney

That all depends on you.

Throughout this book I have given you steps, tools and suggestions to help you implement Profit First for Tradies in your business and help you get your bookkeeping and other systems sorted out. The one thing I can't give you is the will to get stuck in and do this. I can't make you do anything, but I hope this book has given you plenty of examples of other tradies just like you who have successfully put Profit First for Tradies into practice, who have sorted out their bookkeeping and made it efficient, and have come out the other side not only much more profitable but also having changed their lives and the lives of their family.

As we know, running a business is hard work, and I hope reading this book has helped give you some ideas on how to be more efficient and effective in your business so it isn't as difficult as it has been in the past. Once you nail Profit First for Tradies and your business is consistently profitable – which means you are taking the wage or salary you deserve as well as profit to reward you for your grit and determination in starting and running a business – you will be able to look to the future and start planning what you want your life to be like each decade. And you will finally be able to look towards retirement and start planning with confidence.

If you have made it to the end of this book you certainly deserve a huge congratulations. It shows that you are ready to change, that you are ready to do things differently. You understand that doing what you have always done is not going to be enough to get you to where you want to go.

Start making changes today:

- ☐ **Step 1:** Email me at Katie@profitfirstfortradies.com.au with the subject line 'I've finished the book!' I have some additional resources for those who do and I would love to share them with you.

- ☐ **Step 2:** If you haven't already, be sure to join my Facebook group Profit First for Tradies, and join a group of likeminded tradies who are just as keen as you are to make a change.

- ☐ **Step 3:** Your next step is to rank in order of importance which areas of your business you are going to fix first, and then what you will fix next, and so on.

- ☐ **Step 4:** Get started on your first area today.

Remember, you do not have to do everything at once, just do one thing, then the next, and so on. I know it may seem like a long road ahead, but it will certainly be worth it.

You also do not have to do this alone.

GLOSSARY OF KEY TERMS

ATO (Australian Taxation Office): The ATO is the Government's principal revenue collection agency. Their main role is to manage and collect our taxes, such as GST, PAYG and taxes payable when businesses make profits.

CAPs (Current Allocation Percentages): These are the current percentages you use to allocate money to your various accounts. For example, a profit CAP of 5% means that with every allocation you make you will transfer 5% of the balance in your INCOME account to your PROFIT account.

Debt freeze: The debt freeze process is more than just 'no more new debt'. It's a step-by-step process to cut unnecessary expenses and to stop incurring new expenses, as well as finding ways to become more profitable.

Domino your debts: This is the strategy Scott Pape suggests (in his great book *The Barefoot Investor*) to focus and reduce your current debts.

GAAP (Generally Accepted Accounting Principles): These are a set of accounting standards and procedures used by most businesses. GAAP assumes Sales – Expenses = Profit, thereby treating profit as an afterthought.

GST (Good and Services Tax): This is added to nearly everything we sell in Australia. Once you are registered for GST you are required to withhold GST on behalf of the government and remit that amount less the GST you can claim, usually each quarter but for some businesses it may be monthly.

Instant assessment: Income statements and balance sheets can be tedious and confusing. The instant assessment is a tool that gives you a quick, clear view of the current financial health of your business.

OPEX (operating expenses): In the Profit First system, you should be paying all your bills out of your OPEX account.

Pareto Principle: Otherwise known as the 80/20 rule, the Pareto Principle states that 80% of effects come from 20% of causes. In other words, 80% of your revenue tends to come from 20% of your clients. To further boost your revenue, try to replicate and do more business with this top 20%.

Parkinson's Law: C. Northcote Parkinson's adage that work expands to fill the available time is the same tendency your business has to use up all available resources. This is why Profit First suggests to put your profit away first rather than before there is none available.

Preparing for Profit First: An assessment tool used by certified Profit First Professionals for business that may not have full financials available to them or who are new to business.

Primacy effect: Our tendency to place greater emphasis on what we encounter first. In Profit First we believe profit is important and that is why we put profit first.

Profit and loss (P&L): Also known as an income statement, this shows your income and expenses and the profitability of your business over a specific period of time.

Profit assessment: A full assessment of your business based on the Profit First system. A profit assessment gives you a full picture of your business and highlights the areas that are causing greatest concern.

Profit First Professional (PFP): Certified accountants, bookkeepers or coaching professionals who are certified in the Profit First system. To find one, go to www.profitfirstaustralia.com.au.

Real revenue: This is used as an alternative to gross profit. In Australia we have GST and this is taken off first, and for tradies who use subcontractors and/or materials, we subtract those from Income to derive the 'true revenue' (that is, real revenue) that the business generates. In the traditional sense, gross profit can vary based on different interpretations. The objective of real revenue is to simplify the calculations variable.

Sales – Expenses = Profit: The traditional accounting formula that we are going to flip to achieve profitability: Sales – Profit = Expenses.

Survival trap: When you operate your business week to week, you'll find yourself in the survival trap, doing anything to generate revenue, even when it goes against your company's vision and is outside the bounds of your top clients' needs.

TAPs (Target Allocation Percentages): The ideal percentage of revenue you should eventually aim to allocate to Profit, Tax, and Owner's Comp. You will gradually increase your CAPs toward your TAPs.

www.ingramcontent.com/pod-product-compliance
Lightning Source LLC
Chambersburg PA
CBHW071647210326
41597CB00017B/2137